The

Book

of

(Even More)

Awesome

The

Book

of

(Even More)
Awesome

Neil Pasricha

hardie grant books

MELBOURNE · LONDON

Published in 2011 by Hardie Grant Books

Hardie Grant Books (UK)
Dudley House, North Suite
34–35 Southampton Street
London WC2E 7HF
www.hardiegrant.co.uk

Hardie Grant Books (Australia)
85 High Street
Prahran, Victoria 3181
www.hardiegrant.com.au

A catalogue record of this book is available from the British Library.

All photos by Sam Javanrouh (dailydoseofimagery.com) with the exception of "Napping with
somebody else" by Jenny Rigby, "Waking up to the smell of sizzling bacon" by Rich Gidvilas,
"Realizing you still remember your childhood friend's phone number" by Meghan Hughes, "Finally
getting the perfect picture" by Natalie Mazzarelli, "That feeling in your stomach when you go really
high on the swings" by Jeremy Marr, and "The sound of snow crunching under your boots" by Connie
Tsang. Thanks to all of them for their beautiful images.

Cover concept by gray318
Text design by Amada Dewey
Printed in the UK by CPI Cox & Wyman

Hoping and thinking and dreaming and playing and being and living and loving. AWESOME!

The

Book

of

(Even More)

Awesome

So what's this all about?

We're all gonna get lumps.

We're all gonna get bumps.

Nobody can predict the future, but we do know one thing about it: **It ain't gonna go according to plan.**

Yes, we'll all have massive highs, big days, and proud moments. Colour-faded, **postcard-streaked blurs** will float and flash through our brains on our deathbeds, of wide eyes on graduation stages, **father-daughter dances at weddings**, and healthy baby screeches in the delivery room. And dotting those big moments will be smaller ones too: fragile hugs from Grandma on **Christmas morning**, two-year-olds handing you a bouquet of dandelions and saying "I love you," or your boyfriend staring into your eyes **and smiling** while lazing in bed on Sunday morning.

But like I said.

We're all gonna get lumps.

We're all gonna get bumps.

It's sad but things could happen or hurt you that you just can't predict.

Your husband might leave you, **your girlfriend may cheat**, your headaches might be serious, your dog could get smacked in the street. Yes, your kids might get mixed up with tough gangs or bad scenes. It's sad but your mum could get cancer . . . or your dad could get mean.

There will be times in your life you're tossed down the well too. There will be times you'll cry yourself to sleep, **with twists in your stomach**, with holes in your heart. You may wonder if it's all worth it and you may think that it ain't. You may wonder if you can handle it or **you may beg for restraint**.

But when bad news washes over you and when the pain sponges and soaks in, I really hope you feel like you've always got two big choices:

1. You can swish and swirl in gloom and doom forever, or
2. You can grieve and face the future with newly sober eyes

Sure, life has dealt me some blows in the couple of years I've been writing about awesome things. There was the **mind-numbing loneliness** of moving to a brand new nowhere town, the broken heart of a broken marriage, and the searing waves of regret when a friend took his own life.

But I'm lucky because I've had **a way out** for the past two years. I've had a secret pill to swallow, a magic potion to swirl, and a bubbly cauldron to sip from every time I felt down **or felt black** or felt blue. And I hope you know that remedy and I hope you feel it too.

After all, you're reading it right now.

Yes, awesome things make my life better, people. And I hope they do the same for you.

I honestly can't go a day anymore without smiling at a couple of tiny awesome things in my world. Whether it's stepping on barely frozen puddles, **finally peeing after holding it forever**, or driving to an intersection just as the lights turn green, these tiny things make a great big difference.

So come on. Come on! Are you with me? Who's with me? I say if you've got a couple of fist pumps in you, if you've got a **sneaky twinkle in your eye**, if you've got an itchy old soul that loves smiling at strangers, dancing at weddings, and popping the heck out of Bubble Wrap, then come on in and join **The AWESOME Movement**.

It's my sincere hope that awesome things help those of us who need them to grieve and **move on**, and remind us that the best things in life are free. For us, maybe it's a ladder out of the well or a dusty torch beam in the darkness. For others, perhaps it's just a little laugh on the back of the toilet, **a bit of peace before bed**, or a spark for debates about what matters most to you, you, or you.

For me, I know I'll have more dark days, and I know my friends will too, but I like thinking that glue movies, **flavour pockets**, and big night naps will always cheer me through to the other side.

While polar ice caps melt, **while health care debates rage on**, while buzz saws chop down forests, while wars go on and on, I hope there's always a special secret place where we can turn off that bright light, **snuggle right on up**, and get comfy to chat about the sweetest parts of life.

Thank you for reading *The Book of (Even More) Awesome*. I feel so incredibly grateful, lucky, and honoured to walk down this road with you. And thank you for letting our stories all **tightly twist together** as we all keep moving forward and we all keep moving on.

Hope you enjoy the book.

—Neil

Coming back to your own bed after a long trip

Do you remember your **Worst Sleep Ever**?

Man, I sure do. It was back when I was at uni and a few friends and I drove a **skiddy van** across a snowy highway in the middle of a blizzard to crash with my friend Chad. It was a frozen weekend full of laughs and catching up with friends who had all been pulled apart after high school.

Now, it was late Friday night in this quiet university town when a few of us figured it was time to hit the sack. There were no fresh linens, soft pillows, or fluffy towels waiting for us there. Nope, all we had in that cold, dark basement were a **couple of ratty couches**, a hollow wooden door to the blizzard outside, and some cheap ticking clocks on the wall.

Well, what choice did we have?

We made little beds from couch cushions, used jumpers for pillows, and covered our shivering bodies with zippery, snow-smeared winter coats. As if that wasn't bad enough, the clocks **tick-tick-ticked** all night and somebody got home really late and left the back door wide open. Nobody noticed until morning when all our teeth were chattering and there was a **foot-high snowdrift** under the ping-pong table.

It was a nightmare, but I know you've been there too.

Power-napping on bumpy aeroplanes, crashing on **flabby futons** or jabby mattresses, sleeping in rainy forests in leaky tents, you've had your fair share. Bad sleeps, sad sleeps, **sack-pillow heaps**, weird alarm clock beeps, and through it all you enjoy long, fidgety nights of groggy pillow turns and fuzzy blanket burns.

But after those killer sleeps in **nightmare paradise**, it's always a great feeling when you come home to the warm and cozy comfort of your heavenly bed. Yes, you're like a bear scraping together **crinkly leaves** and warm mud for a long winter of hibernation or a **soaring eagle** swooping home from the windy treetops to the twiggy goodness of your comfy nest.

Your dented pillow, warm flannel sheets, and preset alarm clock are waiting for you.

So welcome home, baby.

You made it.

AWESOME!

Sneaking cheaper lollies into the movie theatre

Contraband lollies taste better.

Here's how to make the magic happen:

Step 1: Bag Up. Large handbags come in handy here. Ladies, pull out the fattest potato sack you got and sling it across your shoulder with pride. For everyone else, you can try a bulky backpack or shopping bag. Business folks can pull off the classy briefcase. Mums can use the false bottom of a nappy bag. The only thing to avoid are *Matrix*-style trench coats with burrito dents in all the inside pockets.

Step 2: Food Up. Stuff that puppy with gummy worms, bubble tape, and cinnamon buns. If you're feeling risky, throw in a couple of cold and slippery cans of soft drink, a bag of microwave popcorn, or a pocket flask. Know your limits, though. Steamy meatball subs and hot soups in thermoses are for experts only.

Step 3: Walk Up. Confidence is everything. Hold your head high, strut a mean strut, and you'll be just fine. No ticket ripper should say anything, but if you do happen to get caught you can always pretend you're diabetic. "Honestly, these are prescription lollies."

Step 4: Eat Up. Tear open the bag of chips with your teeth, crack the soft drink during a gunfight, and shake the Nerds during the Spanish dance sequence. Just get in there and get munching.

Get in there and get crunching.
Get in there and get
AWESOME!

Stomping dry crunchy leaves on the footpath

Green baby buds pop out in the spring, healthy leaves **fly high to the sky** all summer, and ageing beauties flash and change colours in autumn. Then they eventually snap off and crack off and **crumble and tumble** down to the footpath.

People, it's true—the sun rose, the sun set, months went by, and the Earth actually **tilted on its axis** before this moment could appear before you.

So smile a big smile on your way to school and enjoy the **crispy crunch** that comes when you walk ten centimetres out of your way to smash a brittle little leaf into smithereens.

AWESOME!

Finally getting that tiny piece of popcorn out of your teeth

You know when you can just feel that **popcorn kernel** stuck back there in the **swampy recesses** of your mouth and it's totally infuriating?

Yes, your tongue slides past its smooth surface unsuccessfully, your toothbrush's **flimsy bristles** just can't shake it, and your fingernails can't pop it from the **tight molar deathgrip**.

So the fork is dropped and the dessert lies unfinished, the conversation fades to a blurry, distant noise, **and the world stops** around you as you keep trying and trying and trying and trying to bust that kernel out. You close your eyes and squint, you tilt your head, you emit a deep-bass *nnnnnnn* sound, as your body directs all available faculties to getting this thing gone. But the dastardly kernel still clings tightly, **clogging and gumming up** your entire system until you're completely frustrated and annoyed beyond belief . . .

Then it suddenly falls out.

Trumpets blast and **angels sing** as your mouth rejoices in a tiny moment of heavenly relief. Now it's time to dive into that cheesecake and rejoin the lost conversation in a beautiful moment of

AWESOME!

Peeling that sticky glue off the back of your new credit card

··

Peel the pleasure.

It doesn't matter if you're a **Smooth Roller** who uses your finger to slowly wheel the sticky icky into a little jelly roll or a **Stretch Inspector** who grabs a glue corner and yanks it further and further until it eventually snaps.

Nope, doesn't matter at all.

Just enjoy the ride.

AWESOME!

Living with someone who doesn't mind killing spiders

···

It's great living with someone who doesn't mind killing spiders.

At uni we would call upon our roommate Dee to take care of the job. It was almost too easy, too. "Dee!" we'd yell from the couch, lazily flipping channels while eating Maggi noodles, "Spider." And that was it, really. Sure enough, every time, Dee's bedroom door would crack open, his **lumbering frame would cast long shadows down the hall**, and he'd step out slowly, raise his eyebrows, and then just go about taking care of business. I always admired his quiet, serious approach to the whole thing. No exchange of pleasantries, no asking for help, no mentioning it later. It was just business with him. Case closed, open and shut. He'd finish up and go back to studying in his room like nothing happened. Life was good.

Then I got married and the role of **Spider Killer** was delegated to me. It's a fair arrangement and I don't mind the responsibility, but I have to tell you: it's a different story when you're the one calmly grabbing a Kleenex from the bathroom on demand, walking over to the spider, squishing it to smithereens, and then flushing it down the toilet to seal the deal. Because that's when it really hits home. That's when you first feel the weight of the spidercide resting squarely on your conscience. It's there and you know it. Eventually you just get numb.

I miss living with Dee. I think I took his role for granted for too long. Looking back, I just want to tell you now: if you currently live with someone who takes care of your spiders, thank them. **Hug them.** Smile and say you appreciate the good work they're doing. Because let me tell you, one day you might be called upon to take their place, and only then will you see what they go through each and every time a Daddy Long-Legs scurries up a wall.

So then, all together now. Let's hear it for them. Living with someone who doesn't mind killing spiders?

AWESOME!

When batteries *are* included

I'm the **Robin Hood** of batteries.

Since I am an extremely cheap person I always rob from the rich battery-filled remotes on my couch and **give to the poor** new gadgets lying on my bench. I stumble around Sherwood Lounge Room, clicking open plastic battery doors, hunting for dependable double-As to get the job done.

Of course, this battery robbery always backfires next time I sit down to watch a flick. I plop onto the couch and pick up the lighter-than-usual remote and then curse my former self for screwing my current self. Then the camera pans to another scene of me stumbling around again, this time **battery-jacking** the poor so I can feed the rich.

It's a terrible, neverending cycle.

That's what makes it special when batteries **are** included. That's what makes it special when you yank open the new Baby Farts-So-Real and there's a small, plastic-wrapped case of cheapo batteries from the **Taiwanese black market** sitting in the box.

Sure, sure, maybe those knockoff Ultra-Power or **Extra-V Vvoltage** batteries don't inspire the most confidence, but whatever man, because surprise batteries are a big win every time.

It's like the company is saying "Come on, let's get going, people."

"First round's on us."

AWESOME!

When it feels like the lyrics to the song you're listening to were written just for you

Maybe a quiet haze drifts in your dorm as you worry about upcoming exams and patchy friendships. Maybe your heart just got flattened by a **runaway relationship** and the knots in your stomach are twisting and burning. Or maybe you're trekking cross-country with a backpack and a dream and are suddenly **sucker-punched** with a jabby stab of loneliness.

When you're pumped up, **pumped down**, shaken sideways, or rattled around, it's always comforting to share a moment with a song that perfectly reflects your mood. Sometimes it seems like they're singing right to you.

So come on and smile along, **nod quietly with the song**, and push ahead, plow forward, and keep soldiering right on.

AWESOME!

Correctly guessing if the door is push or pull

....

Doors can be trouble.

Strutting to the shopping centre, **strolling to the shop**, you spy those glassy doubles in the distance just waiting for you to size them up and give them a big push or pull.

Sure, it looks easy, but we all know it's nothing but.

Nope, thanks to years of tense negotiations, backroom deals, and political infighting, the **International Alliance for Door Design Consistency** has reached a suffocating stalemate in its goal of coming up with one door we can all understand. So while those corporate bigwigs give each other evil eyes in smoky boardrooms **We The People** are left figuring it out on the front lines, door by door, day by day.

It sucks when you make the wrong move too. Pull a push or push a pull and you're suddenly five years old again with wide eyes, **untied laces**, and thick boogers snaking down your upper lip.

Yes, that's why swinging open a confusing door on the first try is such a great high. You just saved yourself a **horrible second of humiliation** and are now coasting smoothly through life in the fast lane.

AWESOME!

When a cop finally passes you after driving behind you for a while

....

Cruising cops cause traffic stops.

Yes indeedy, we law-aspiring citizens immediately slow to a **speed limit cruise** when we spot cops silently swerving behind our bumpers. We're the jittery **school of fish** with jumpy eyes and they're the silent shark swimming over to our lane.

With our hearts drum-thumping and our **white-knuckled hands** gripping the wheel, we temporarily become **Super Drivers**—using our signals, leaving space, and checking our mirrors every two seconds.

We don't know if the cop is eyeballing us, about to **flick his flashers**, or typing our number plate into his computer, so we're in a heightened bug-eyed state. Seconds tick by like hours when **Yourtown's Finest** stick to our heels and force questions through our brains: Was I actually speeding? Should I change lanes? Does he want me to speed up?

Everything slowly and slowly builds and builds to a bigger and bigger feeling of tension and pain . . .

. . . until he finally just zooms off into the distance, never to be heard from again.

AWESOME!

When you learn a new word and then suddenly start seeing it everywhere

You know how it goes: something weird like *coagulate*, *vexed*, or *perforated* leaps into your temporal lobe and wedges itself there tightly, grabbing a beer, **putting its feet up**, making itself at home.

But then soon magazine articles are zooming the word up to your eyeballs, your uni professor is **dropping it in lectures**, and you see it hanging strangely coagulate in the middle of a random book.

"I never knew that word before," you think, "but now it's following me around."

See, the **Lords of Language** know you well. They gotta repeat things to seal in the learning. So when it happens just enjoy that personal thrill, **feel the connection crackle**, and smile and nod because you just got a little bit smarter and a lot more

AWESOME!

When the dog's really excited you're back home

....

Greasy forehead, sore ankles, and a dull headache cap your **traffic-jammy** ride home from a long day at work. Dragging yourself to the door, you picture the **bland burrito** you're gonna nuke for dinner as your stomach rumbles and grumbles.

Yeah, the day got you down, the day knocked you out, but suddenly you unlock the door and your mood **zooms sky-high** as there's a loving and waiting BARK BARK BARK BARK BARK BARK BARK BARK BARK!!!

Someone's happy to see you.

AWESOME!

Dancing when you're home alone

Get your groove on long.

Get your groove on strong.

After all, maybe you're hanging with a heavy heart, **burning with a hot temper**, or snowed in after a bad day. If there's a black cloud hanging over your head, there's no cheaper cure than having a **solo dance party** in the comfort of your place.

Just lock that door, **shutter those blinds**, and crank the bumping thumping music, baby. Because it's time to get down with the get down:

- **The Microphone**. Wooden spoons are ideal but there are good substitutes like toothbrushes, Swiffer dusters, or hair dryers. Just don't trip on the cord.
- **The Crowd**. It's all about mirrors. Nod and let them nod right back at you. Watch them mouth the words and raise their fists with yours. What a beautiful audience.
- **The Critics**. There are none! This is the best part. Nobody says you're singing out of key so just wail till you can't wail no more. For bonus points get

your voice so loud and dirty it scratches the back of your throat.

- **The Wardrobe**. You've got a few costume options including the classic ripped raggedy T-shirt and pair of faded track pants. There's also underwear only or even full-on lounge room nude. Relax, you look great. Time to rock out.

Yes, we've all been home alone and sometimes it's fun to spin your head into the moment. So come on and turn it on, **crank it up**, and just shake it baby, shake it baby, shake it like that.

AWESOME!

Getting tucked in

Bedtime is terrible.

TV flicks off, **friends go home**, sun dips down, and you're all alone.

But just before you fall asleep sometimes there's a little treat.

Just before you drift to dreams sometimes there's a little scene.

Just before you fade away sometimes there's a little left to say.

Mum or dad slips through your door, **they sit and smile on your bed**, and then they swipe your shaggy hair right across your forehead. They smooth out the covers and squeeze them up to your chin as they smile and ask how your day has been.

Sometimes there's a story, **sometimes there's a book**, sometimes there's just smiling, sometimes there's a look. But no matter what, we all know that tiny moment of cozy comfort always feels like a warm and loving moment of

AWESOME!

The sound of a solid crack from a good break in billiards

....

I am a terrible pool player.

Yet, despite this, whenever someone at a bar asks me to play against them or be their partner, I'm like sure, yeah, **I'm totally in**.

I mean, I'm having a good time, **I'm in a good mood**, so I sort of tipsily swagger over to the cue rack on the wall and pretend to be sizing them up. **"Oh man, all the good ones are gone,"** I always say extremely loudly, my eyes darting around at the other players with a sad little "Yeah, it's true" head nod, being careful to plant seeds of disappointment early so nobody expects me to actually sink a ball.

After that, I begin a desperate search for chalk. "Gotta have some chalk, gotta have some chalk," I'll mumble, as I walk in circles around the pool table, looking underneath it and in all the pockets until I find some. And when I do, **I really go to town**. Honestly, I rub my pool cue in that chalk and twist it around tightly, and then I flare the edges to cover up all the missed spots.

If all goes according to plan, I'll keep chalking my cue until somebody breaks. The goal here is to avoid eye contact until the game starts, because otherwise I might be asked to break, and that's never a pretty sight.

No, the four or five times I've foolishly agreed to kick off the game ended up embarrassing everyone involved. I'll generally skid the cue off the side of the cue ball, sending it wildly spinning directly into a side pocket. Or I'll get under the ball by accident and send it flying across the bar, where it'll softly roll up against the boot of some **ponytailed, tattooed biker dude**, who will then shoot me a cold, piercing stare and begin punching his fist into his palm.

No, it's better for everyone if I avoid the break. Frankly, I shouldn't even be playing.

But what I will do is peek up from my obsessive chalking so that I can watch the break, because I love the break, because the break is great. I mean, it's an explosive crack that rises above the background bar buzz and captures everyone's attention as the balls fly in all directions.

The sound of a solid crack from a good break in billiards is the sound of **a good fifteen to twenty minutes of fun** getting started. And it's the sound of people enjoying themselves with a couple of drinks, some good friends, and a great night.

And that sounds a lot like

AWESOME!

When a baby falls asleep on you

You're a human pillow.

Feel that tiny heart beating on your chest, that strawberry-sized hand **gripping your finger**, and those baby powder breaths softly whispering in and out . . .

When you were a **little baby** you fell asleep on people all the time. Now that you're all grown up you're helping another life on its way. And just think: One day way off in the distance this **softly sleeping snuggler** will be doing the exact same thing for someone else.

AWESOME!

Giant morning stretches accompanied by stupid noises

Crack that back.

Everybody's got their own gorilla jungle noises when they wake up in the morning. Here's a few famous moves for waking up your bones:

1. **The Insane Wiggle.** This one's the classic. There's no focus and direction here—you're just twisting and turning in a crumpled lump of sheets and twisted blankets. Maybe you squeeze your face into your pillow, pull your legs into your chest, or just let out some long deep grunts to feel the stretchy buzz in the small of your back.

2. **The Starfish.** This is where you lie in bed and stretch your arms up to the sides and your legs down and out. The starfish works best if your girlfriend's out of town or you manage to land a night in a king-size hotel bed by yourself. Arty nerds might refer to this move as The Vitruvian Man.

3. **The Old Man Can Walk Again.** When I lived in Boston, my roommate Joey was famous for this. You'd hear his bedroom door creak open and he'd slowly

inch out—hunched over in a stained undershirt and baggy boxers, blindly touch-feeling his way to the bathroom without his glasses on. Eventually he'd give a few wheezy groans and stretch up like he was getting out of his wheelchair for the first time in years.

4. **The Yogi Master**. These people actually do real stretches when they wake up. They might even throw their hair in a ponytail, lay down a mat, and jump into a tight black unitard.

5. **The Cobra**. Here's where you stretch your spine out by leaning up like a cobra. For full effect make sure to throw a few hisses and menacing head fakes at your sleeping husband.

6. **The Safety Stretch**. Your bed buddy is sleeping in a little later so you're careful not to wake them up. Watch the grunts, watch the groans, and stretch out nice and quietly, people. Sure, it's not as rewarding a stretch but it beats accidentally punching them in the temple while they're drooling and dreaming.

7. **The Ballet Dancer**. Prop one foot up on the radiator and lean forward like you're about to hit the stage. (Tutu optional but recommended.)

8. **The Dog Leg**. That big dog stretch sends all your molecules zooming around so fast that one leg just starts pounding the mattress uncontrollably. Your

thumping dog leg lets you know the stretch is working.

Now, no matter your style, it sure feels great to stretch that spine, get the blood flowing, and pop all your bones into place.

Bring on the day!

AWESOME!

Glue movies

....

What's your glue movie?

For me, I'm completely sucked in anytime I accidentally stumble on *A League of Their Own* while flipping channels. Yes, watching Tom Hanks and Geena Davis scratch out wins on the diamond always hooks me like a fish till the credits roll.

See, glue movies are **any movie you can't stop watching whenever you see it on TV.**

Nope, don't matter how many times you've seen 'em, don't matter if you own 'em, don't matter if you don't—just forget the laundry, **skip the dishes**, and make your lunch tomorrow. You're stuck in a glue movie so start popping corn and pouring soft drinks because you're not going anywhere.

Now, I was chilling in my friends Nick and Julie's basement apartment one night when we started chatting about glue movies. After I spent five minutes spilling **potato chip crumbs** all over my T-shirt while describing Madonna and Rosie O'Donnell's on-field chemistry, Nick started up a rant of his own.

"You know, you would think my glue movie would be *The Usual Suspects*," he began. "I can pick it up anywhere and knowing the twist makes every scene more interesting. Like, what's true, what's made up? I've seen it twenty times and I still don't know. But then again, it's **completely unwatchable** when edited for television. In the police lineup scene they say something like 'Hand me the keys, you very large cockroach.' It's awful. So . . . now that I think about it, my glue movie is definitely *Heat*. Long movie, understated performance by De Niro, best bank-robbing scene in history, and enough relationship stuff so Julie gets into it."

It was a good argument and Nick was satisfied with it. He took a **long swig** of his drink and nodded his head a little bit as he came to terms with his glue movie selection. Then there was a pause while I licked my fingers and fished out the **last crumby triangle of potato chips** from my chip bag before Julie went off like a rocket:

"My movie is definitely *The Mighty Ducks 2*," she started, excitedly. Nick and I raised eyebrows, but she ramped up. "Look, I'm smiling just thinking about it. I had a crush on all the boys from the first movie, but now I can only responsibly love them closer to the **legal age of consent**. Plus, they had a girl on the team and I always dreamed of being that female hero. And I generally love movies with kids because they remind you of actors before they were big. I mean, I loved **Joshua Jackson** in *Dawson's Creek* because of the ducks," she finished.

Nick shrugged and nodded, I furrowed my eyebrows and gave a tentative thumbs-up, but Julie wasn't quite done.

"Oh yeah!" She beamed. "And the movie taught me everything I know about hockey, which can be summarised in three words: **Ducks fly together.** This is what I yell whenever I walk by and Nick's watching it on TV."

We smiled and laughed because it was clear these movies really do hold a special place in our hearts.

Maybe you're glued to the screen waiting for the redemption in *Shawshank*, nervous for the courtroom drama in *My Cousin Vinny*, or eager for the final Quidditch match in *Harry Potter*.

But no matter what, watching your glue movie is like hanging out with an old friend who pops by for an unexpected visit. After you pour a drink and settle into your **couch dent**, the memory pops and nostalgia drops start sparking and sizzling in your brain. Suddenly you're reminded of drives to the shopping centre in mum's minivan, crashing on basement couches with friends, or sharing old faves with a new flame.

So get stuck in your glue movies and just enjoy them, everybody.

They'll be yours forever.

AWESOME!

Watching milk go into coffee

Swirling seas of milky white twist and twirl like **strange and distant galaxies** in the far corners of outer space. As you grab a rushed coffee break in the chatty workplace kitchen or cutlery-clinking dining hall, just stare deeply into your chipped ceramic **telescope** and enjoy the two-second escape from reality to watch those floating clouds mix and melt deep into the swirling darkness.

AWESOME!

When the hiccups stop

How do you get rid of a bad case of **The Hics**?

Brother, I don't know about you, but in my neck of the woods it's all about the **junk science techniques**. Yes, when your diaphragm starts seizing, it's time to keep cool, keep calm, keep collected, and try one of these:

1. **The Backwards Sip.** Tilt your chin to your chest and drink upside down from the wrong side of a glass of water. Wet fringe, stinging eyes, and a drippy forehead mean you did it right.

2. **Sugar, Spice, and Everything Nice.** Some people say eating a spoonful of sugar or gargling with sugar water helps. Hey, any cure that sounds delicious works for me, so I say give it a shot. While you're at it, try scoffing a couple of Kit-Kats for that bum knee and chugging a few cans of Coke for that eyelash stuck in your eye.

3. **The Surprise Attack.** This is when you think someone scaring you will frighten the hiccups away. Of course, popping a paper bag behind you or clapping in your ear isn't going to cut it. No, this only works when somebody shoves you off a tall sky-

scraper ledge onto a properly rigged-up safety net forty stories below.

4. **The Deep-Sea Diver.** Fill your lungs up, pop your belly out, and hold your breath as long as possible. If all goes according to plan, your face will look hilarious to all your friends.

Now, come on, let's face facts: None of these usually works so you're stuck pulling off **The Annoying Wait**. You think they're gone, but they're not, and then you think they're gone again, but then they're actually not again, and then you think they're really gone for sure this time.

And then they actually are.

And in that beautiful moment you just stare up at everybody around you with a sweaty face, tired eyes, and a slow smile curling onto your face. Because when the hiccups finally stop, it's a giant swooshing sensation of sweet relief and a great big moment of

AWESOME!

Finding something you lost a long time ago after you already gave up looking for it

....

It happened late one night.

Cruising down the highway, heading home from the airport, my friend Shiv absentmindedly rifled through my passenger-side door full of old computer-printed directions, **parking stubs**, and cracked CD cases.

"What's this?" she asked, popping open a flimsy case and pulling out a dusty, scratched-up mix CD. "It just has the date marked on it with a Sharpie. Uh, let's see, what happened on November 8, 2008?"

"No way!" I said, glancing to my side and seeing one of my favourite mixes ever, which I thought I lost two years ago. My mind suddenly flashed back to **late summer nights** zooming up the highway to my parents' place listening to those tunes after long nights with lost loves . . .

But isn't it always like that?

Finding something you lost long ago after you gave up looking for it is such a great high because you already lived through the emotions:

Phase 1: The Alarm. This is when your sunglasses or bus pass first go missing. It hits you like a rubber mallet to the forehead when you first realise it's gone. Poof, just like that, as if your digital watch or favourite pen grew legs and bolted out of town.

Phase 2: The Search. Next you organise the neighbours and head into the foggy night holding lanterns and pitchforks and linking elbows while you comb the cornfields until dawn. The next few days are a blurry haze of sleepless nights as you lie on a blanket on the damp riverbank watching the police boats drag the bottom for clues.

Phase 3: The Grieve. The trawler nets can't locate your mobile phone or favourite glittery lip gloss so you're forced to face facts and come to grips with reality. It's gone, gone, gone like the wind, and now all that remains are long rambly stories late at the bar and lonely nights sobbing into your pillow.

People, I know it hurts, but we've all been there.

After you've lost, searched, and come up empty, you move on. Time helps, **distance helps**, but the memories never disappear. You try downloading songs from the mix tape and piecing them back together, and you buy a new digital camera with an **empty memory card** to replace the one you lost with a full one.

But it's just never the same.

    . . . until one day

        . . . a long time later

            . . . when you least expect it

                . . . the thing you lost comes back!

Yes, while unzipping the **side pocket of your travel bag** you suddenly spot the diamond earrings that went missing after your cousin's wedding four years ago. While reaching into the bowels of your **messy boot** looking for a torch, you suddenly tug on a **jumper sleeve** that's been buried under a set of golf clubs since summer. And after you slim down and toss on the sassy blazer you wore to prom, guess what's hanging out in that inside pocket? Brother, it's your **crumpled tie** or that wind-up disposable camera with half the film used up from the big night.

When this happens, your eyes pop and **your jaw drops** because you can hardly believe you're seeing your old friend's face right in front of you again. Chills rocket up your spine, love sucker-punches your chest, and **big salty tears** well in the corners of your eyes before streaming like hot rivers down your chubby cheeks.

You laugh, sniffle, and shake your head before giving the person beside you a big hug and smiling up at the world. Clouds part, **bugles blare**, and everything suddenly fills up with the giant swelling sensation of

AWESOME!

Riding home with a box of pizza on your lap

Pepperoni fumes fill the air as mum swerves and curves you home. Yes, that **hot bulky square** of cardboard filled with bubbling mozzarella heats your legs and gets your stomach rumbling for a delicious dinner that nobody needs to cook.

AWESOME!

Picking the fastest moving line at the supermarket checkout

....

You can do it.

Motor around filling your basket with food before spying the checkouts and picking your poison. Here's five tips for living life in the fast lane:

1. **Skip your greens.** Stay away from trolleys full of strange produce. Anyone with tiny bags of coriander or parsley is a guaranteed slowdown because they'll force cashiers to look up codes.

2. **Saving spaces, angry faces.** Watch out for the single guy holding a cake. Sure, he may look like a quick checkout, but he also could be saving a spot for a big-wheeling partner who's about to cruise around the corner with a stuffed trolley. If he's glancing around nervously, avoid the line.

3. **Bag the bagger.** I hate to break it to you but you're terrible at bagging. Sorry, but look at you—wedging frozen peas beside fresh bread, setting potatoes on eggs, making one bag really heavy and one bag really light. No, you've got to leave bagging to the

pros. Make sure you grab a line with a bagger to get the job done right.

4. **Take a flyer on the flyer.** Customers holding dog-eared flyers are probably going to ask questions or slowly tear out coupons. Just remember this handy line: "Flyer in tow? That line is slow." Amen, sing it to your mama.

5. **Mo' cashiers, mo' problems.** We're looking for quick hands, firm credit card swiping, and purposeful change drawer slamming in cashiers. Avoid lanes with two of them because one's in Training Mode. Support their development silently and catch them when they've learned how to double-bag.

Yes, picking the fastest moving line at the supermarket is such a great high. When you get it right, you're like the **undercover cop** of the shop—spying on customers, **eyeballing cashiers**, and swooping in smartly to get the job done in style. AWESOME!

Getting a hug from someone you didn't know you were in a hug relationship with

....

My dad's a side hugger.

When I go see him at my parents' place in the burbs, I usually go in for a quick hello or handshake when I'm popping in the door. But my dad's a **slippery senior** and he always scoots sideways to squeeze my shoulder, bump hips, and smile his soft, goofy smile through **thick boxy glasses** just to tell me he's happy I'm here.

Now, the funny thing about my dad's side hugging is that it's pretty much his only greeting for everybody. Hello! You're getting a side hug. Goodbye! You're getting a side hug. Neighbours, nephews, nobodies: Don't matter who you are, **don't matter why you're here**, you're getting a side hug. My dad upgrades everybody to side hugs and he's proud of it.

I like watching people's faces when they realise their handshake is mutating before their eyes. Sure, they go for the shake, but my dad suddenly scoots sideways before they know it. When that handshake changes, I notice their face changes too. It goes from a polite thin-lipped smile and eyebrow raise to a **full-on toothy grin**. They relax and dissolve into the moment for a second and let the power of touch and **hallway love** remind them that we're all pretty close out there and, come on, we're all in this big thing together.

Getting a hug from someone you didn't know you had a hug relationship with reminds you somebody cares about you. Sometimes it's good to skip the high fives and handshakes.

Sometimes . . . it's just good to hug.

AWESOME!

That one person who laughs when you tell a really bad joke

This is also known as **The Pity Laugh** and it somehow manages to save your terrible joke from being a complete bomb. See, now you didn't serve up a dud that hit dead air. No, no, your humour is just a little **highbrow** and hard to understand, that's all.

AWESOME!

Letting go of the petrol pump perfectly so you end on a round number

I hate $19.98.

When I'm pumping my car full of some sweet-smelling gasoline, I always get tense when I'm **two cents** away from a nice, round number. Maybe I've got a **twenty-dollar bill** in my pocket or maybe I'm throwing it on a credit card. Either way, I just can't be that satisfied with a $20.01 pump. If I hit $20.03 or $20.04, it's like I wasn't even paying attention. Call me **Slow Hands** at that point, because I clearly have no idea what I'm doing.

But if the opposite happens, if I tap that handle ever so sweetly and let a **little thimble** of gasoline drip into my tank so the numbers curl up to twenty bucks even, then it's time to high five the passengers, call the papers, and get ready for a beautifully changeless transaction.

For a split second you transform.

Gone is mum driving the kids home from ballet, gone is the **pizza driver** doing a quick fill before midnight, gone is the suit pumping a fast one before riding the expressway to the office downtown.

Gone, gone, they're all just gone.

People driving by will squint at those pumps and swear they noticed something. Kids staring out the back of the **station wagon** will turn to each other and drop their jaws. Later on, newspaper reporters will write down eyewitness accounts from old folks on the porch across the street. "It must have been my imagination," they'll say. "But I swear I saw someone dressed all in black."

If you let go of the petrol pump at just the right moment, they're talking about you.

Because you are **The Pump Ninja**.

AWESOME!

Finding a parking spot right at the front of the shopping centre just before Christmas

I'm a terrible parker.

Yes, I'm the guy who does a **five-point turn** to get into the spot and a twenty-second slow-mo reverse to get out. I'm the one bumping your bumper at the **speed of sloth** and the one craning my neck wildly to make sure our mirrors don't smash when I pull up beside you.

Since I know my limits behind the wheel I usually head straight for the farthest parking spot in the car park. I'm fine parking under the dim lamp by the **swampgrass** because for me it means no parking stress and no parking problems. I'm alone in my empty parking zone, baby.

Now, when that shopping centre's busy and bumping it's another story.

When those spots all fill up I'm a stressed-out incher-upper, nervously crawling the car park like a **giant tortoise** slowly teetering into the forest to die. Yes, I foolishly follow people with bags only to watch as they toss them in the boot and head back inside. I steer slowly past busy front doors and get caught in pedestrian traffic jams. I creep down entire aisles full of cars and get fooled over and over by **Motorbike Mirages**.

It's pathetic.

But that's what makes it so great when I suddenly find a free parking spot right near the front of the shopping centre. That's when the sun shines **shooting beams of light** at the tiny rectangular oasis of bumpy asphalt before me.

I signal quickly and clog up lanes as I fumble back and forth into the spot, screeching and scraping my tyres with every turn. But once I'm there I hop right out and smile back to stare at the best parking spot in the car park.

AWESOME!

Getting through right away when you call a big company

Thank you for calling.

We are experiencing lower than normal call volumes.

AWESOME!

Eating the last piece
of anything

....

Occasionally, a kind soul will come over to a barbecue toting
a homemade dessert made from some combination of apples,
brown sugar, brownie batter, toffee bits, marshmallows, cher-
ries, and oatmeal. They set their heavy glass dish down on
my kitchen bench and peel back the plastic bag to reveal an
earth-toned rainbow of deliciosity. We gaze at its beauty for
a moment, but then look at the pile of **cold weenies** and bulk
pack of **macaroni salad** lying on the bench and walk away,
knowing that we'll get to that dessert later, just as soon as we
fill our stomachs with all the cheap stuff everyone else
picked up from the clearance rack.

And eventually the end of the meal arrives and the hero
dessert is paraded to the table with pomp, fanfare, forks, and
a stack of plates. But by now everyone is stuffed, and so while
people dip into this **rectangle of tastiness**, they just don't have
room to send the dish back empty. It inevitably gets cling-
wrapped and put in the fridge for leftovers, hasty promises
made to return to it another time.

And that's when it gets interesting. I'm a pretty big fan
of dessert. I like its style. **I think it's cool.** And so I eat it as soon
as possible. I have a piece here, I have a piece there. It re-

places bread the next morning at breakfast, starch the next evening at dinner. I chip away at it until eventually there is only one piece left. And it is the consumption of that last piece, that final, beautiful square of leftover homemade dessert, that is always the sweetest.

See, by this point it's an old friend. I know its taste well, having succumbed to its **viselike grip** over me for a few days since the party. I may actually be sick of it, but I would never admit it. All I know is that there are only a couple more minutes left of enjoying its company forever.

It is a very happy yet very sad time.

There are some ways that eating the last remaining piece of dessert can be made sweeter, though:

1. **Eating it cold.** When that dessert is only a couple of centimetres away from your mouth, there really is no time allowed for heating. (+5 points)
2. **Eating it straight from the big serving dish.** This is tricky, because if you're watching TV you need to awkwardly lift a three-kilo glass dish with one hand so you can shovel the dessert into your mouth with the other. Watch out for wobbling. (+10 points)
3. **Methodically scraping every last crumb, ring of dried icing, and molecule of congealed syrup out of the dish, even using a spatula if you have to.** Licking is optional here but may be necessary. (+15 points)

4. **The big one.** Thinking about the dessert just before you're about to fall asleep or when you wake up in the middle of the night to go to the bathroom, thinking about it and not being able to get it out of your head until you walk to the kitchen, your feet freezing on the cold linoleum, touch-grabbing your way through the black maze of your apartment, until you pop open that refrigerator door, its bright light beaming out at you like the gates of heaven opening, and you just grab that cling-wrapped slice of greatness and eat it right on up. (+100 points)

   AWESOME!

Slowing down

Time is an illusion.

Baby, we're all just spinning, gninnips, spinning.

Electrons spinning in our tall, fleshy bodies, spinning on our **big, wet rock,** spinning in our bright, white solar system, spinning in our **deep, dark galaxy,** spinning in our brain-bustingly big universe.

This neverending **swirly-twirly headtrip** can be a bit much sometimes, so we try to place some delicate order on our bumpy, chaotic lives. We tack calendars on our kitchen cabinets with **organised checkerboards** of days and weeks and months. We make plans for Saturday night, sleep in on Sunday, and head to work Monday morning. See, now instead of swirling and twirling, we've got minutes and hours and days and weeks and months and years and lives.

Oh sure, maybe setting a calendar on the **beautiful insanity** of life is like placing a square of tissue paper on a hurricane. But without the structure and routine we'd just sort of wander around aimlessly forever, you know what I mean?

"Hey man, when you gonna finish uni?"

"Dude, I dunno, maybe when my beard touches my knees?"

No, no, no, we need order, we want order, **we crave order,** we love order.

Order gives us birthdays, anniversaries, and hair appointments. Order gives us the recess bell, **cake-baking smell**, and Christmas Eve with the family. Order gives us library readings, holiday greetings, and long weekends in the summer.

Order gives us a lot.

But sometimes it's great to slow down and get swirly-twirly anyway.

Sometimes it's great to set up a **crinkly tent** on the damp edge of a gushing river and camp out under the stars with someone you love. Sometimes it's great to shutter in and veg out on the **stained corduroy couch** during a snowy weekend at school. Sometimes it's great to slap on baggy khaki shorts and a bright shirt and fly to a distant island just to lie on a hot, sandy beach in front of the **blue, glittery ocean**.

Sometimes it's great to step back and stare at the clouds and sky.

Sometimes it's great to let your thoughts float free and float high.

Sometimes it's great to close your eyes and let it all just slip away.

Sometimes it's great to forget the clock and dream a dream today.

AWESOME!

Taking your high heels off at the end of the night and walking home in bare feet

Give your tired, aching soles a soothing break after a long day of painful slave labour.

It just feels like sweet release.

Or so I've heard.

AWESOME!

When you suddenly remember it's a long weekend

....

Monday is the new Sunday. First off, your TV-watching schedule is messed up. The baseball game was last night so now you're flipping past *Wheel of Fortune* and sitcom re-runs. But no big deal, because even though the night before school or work is a bit of a drag, you can at least rest knowing you've got a four-day week ahead.

Sunday is the new Saturday. Now you can make late night plans without excuses. No sister-in-laws zipping up nappy bags and tying kids' shoelaces in the front hallway at 8:30 p.m. this time. Nope, on long-weekend Sundays the party's just getting started, so toss the seven-year-old on the bed full of jackets and get back to rocking.

Saturday is Uncharted Territory. This is the Bermuda Triangle of the long weekend. You've got two more days to finish your algebra homework, plant the tulip bulbs, or mow the lawn, so that all falls off the radar. Yes, today's the day for a glue movie marathon, long drive to see the grandkids, or late night out with your old friends from high school.

When you suddenly remember it's a long weekend it's time for some head spins. Your brain races with possibilities ahead and you're filled with a tingly buzz of excitement. Yes, you ran up the **bumpy hills** of Monday and Tuesday, scraped by a muddy Wednesday, and clawed through the **frozen tundra** of Thursday and Friday.

Now you're at the top of the mountain breathing the fresh air of the long weekend.

And it is glorious.

AWESOME!

When two biscuits melt together in the oven

....

If you're lucky the edges of both biscuits had a little bit of burn time to harden and brown before congealing into **one giant Siamese biscuit masterpiece**. Now they're stuck together in a crispy brown sugar suture that becomes your mouth-watering reward for baking a big beautiful batch of
AWESOME!

The Moon

Everyone loves the sun. Plants, light, tan lines, we get it, we get it. But, you know what? Today's the day to give props to that other big guy floating up in the sky. Yes, we say the Moon's worth respecting for a few big reasons:

1. **Lights up the night.** Sure, the moon isn't as bright as the sun but he's still a friendly torch on dark nights. If you've ever been lost on a boy scout trip in the forest, driven down a pitch-black country road, or taken a midnight pee at the campsite, you know what we're talking about. Smile as those flickery white shadows glimmer off twigs and branches to help you avoid tumbling down the rocky cliffside.

2. **Turns the tides.** The moon's constant gravitational yanking gives us choppy ocean tides all day long. Tides allow some species to lay eggs, others to ride the waves, and, most importantly, add important time pressures to sand castle competitions. Without them our oceans—and indeed, our lives— would be flat and dreary.

3. **Get out of late free card.** There's something beautiful about seeing the moon hanging around a clear blue morning sky. It's kind of like that coffee shop employee who chills behind the counter after her shift, pouring a few more drinks in her winter jacket before heading home. "Yeah, yeah, I know the sun's here," she seems to say. "Just want to make sure everything's cool before I take off." Also, as everyone knows, it's impossible to be late for work when the moon's still out because it's not officially daytime yet. Be sure to check your Rules of Life handbook if you need clarification on this important matter.

4. **Toss the Timex.** The moon's waxing and waning keep our dates in check, thank you very much. According to our egghead pals at Wikipedia the moon even formed the basis of the world's first calendars with 13,000-year-old eagle-bone relics dug up in Le Placard, France. That's why our current months are estimates of the lunar cycle and why "moon" and "month" are from the same root. Word to your dictionary.

5. **Let's get nuts.** Both "lunacy" and "loony" are derived from "Luna", the Latin name for the Moon. Ancient googly-eyed nerds Aristotle and Pliny the Elder thought full moons made people nuts because our brains are mostly water and therefore we

get the same Earth–Moon tidal forces in our heads. Well, the jury's still out on that one, but there's nothing wrong with a bit of spice in life. So when that full moon comes around, feel free to bulge your eyeballs, act like a caveman, or wear your wacky purple tie to the office meeting.

Sometimes our home planet can seem like a lonely base, spinning in place, floating through space. But when you stare out your bedroom window, up into the distant forever reaches of infinite darkness, remember we've got a friend riding with us everywhere we go. Yes, the Moon's our lunchtime pal in the giant universal playground and our seatmate at the back of the big bang bus. So when it seems like the big blackness is lonely, when it seems like we're far from home, well just remember that the Moon's always beside us... as we ride into the deep unknown.

AWESOME!

The moment after you wake up from a nightmare and suddenly realise it was all just a dream

With a dropped jaw, buggy eyes, and sweaty palms, your **hot, salty head** pops up from your warm pillow in a heart-pounding state of emergency. After a second of **massively intense panic** where you zoom into brain-rushing, adrenaline-gushing overdrive, it suddenly just dawns on you . . .

It was all just a dream.

It was all just a dream.

It was all just a dream.

AWESOME!

Pain

....

It's there for a reason.

Whether you're shredding your legs on a raspberry bush, **scalding your hand in hot water**, or taking an arrow to the chest in the forest, I got bad news for you, brother: **That's gonna hurt**. Yes, when our bodies take blows, those powerful jolts make us cry salty tears, run for the hills, or crash-land in hospital beds with limbs hanging everywhere.

But that pain really is there for three big reasons:

1. **Stop! . . . Bandage time.** The first thing pain does is make you stop doing that painful thing you're doing. Your brain focuses every neuron on getting you out of Danger Bay and returning you to Safety Beach. Stop! You're lawnmowering your foot. Stop! You're leaning on an oven burner. Stop! You're dancing in much too baggy pants.
2. **Long live the cast.** Pain reminds us to take care of injured body parts so they can heal. We lean on crutches so our ankles can untwist, plaster broken arms so bones can set, and bandage cuts to prevent infections. Throbbing migraines send us to dark rooms and bum knees get us limping because

that's what we **need**, sister. Pain's just whispering
advice to send us down the road to good health.

3. **Fool me twice, shame on me**. Pain's whole plan is
   to get us to stop doing painful things long term.
   Think of pain as a cranky granny shaking her
   finger when you sheepishly come schlepping up
   the front walk battered and bruised. "No more
   running through raspberry bushes, mister," she
   starts. "No more checking hot water with your
   fingers. And no more medieval battle games in
   the forest."

Now, if all that wasn't enough, **our egghead pals** over at
Wikipedia even report that people who don't feel pain actually live shorter lives. Maybe that's because pain's just there
to do a job for us. It motivates us to flee hurtin' scenes, pro-
tects our body while it heals, and teaches us to avoid painful
places in the future.

Pain's our invisible Life Coach, **sewn into our bones**,
twisted in our DNA, and helping us all keep strong as we
keep motoring on.

AWESOME!

The smell of an old hardware shop

....

Let's go on a trip.

It's time to walk into an old hardware shop and take a look around. There's a dusty, paint-splotched radio playing oldies, a Cash Only sign above the till, and an old man with glasses and heavy plaid shirt leaning on the counter just daring you to ask him a question he can't answer. As you walk past the tired vending machine with soft drinks below market prices you take a big whiff and bring back a brainful of love and memories with these gems:

- **Tyres**. Chinese chemical plants, hot liquid rubber, and the musty stench of cargo bays combine to form this mind-altering buzz. And when you cruise on by don't forget to grab a free hand massage by rubbing your palm across all those tiny plastic hairy bits sticking out in all directions.

- **Those tightly packed piles of soil**. Flopped sideways and drooping in all directions, don't these bags always look like they're about to burst at the seams? Well, I guess the problem is that some of them do, leaking their sweet-smelling brown-with-white-flecks load all over the floor.

- **The key-cutting machine**. If your hardware shop is lucky enough to have a kid working away on a screaming key-cutting machine, then you're probably sniffing in some oily machine parts and hot metal scraps flying in all directions.
- **Stacks of lumber**. Decades of sun, water, and carbon dioxide help grow tiny seedlings in the sod into majestic giants of the forest. Now, even though they're diced into bits, they're still exhaling those deep woody, sappy-fresh scents.
- **Assorted old spills**. Somebody kicked a can of paint thinner under Aisle 3 fifteen years ago and now its faintly toxic aroma is hanging limply in the air along with metal nail dust, shiny tools, and plastic snow shovels.
- **Big plastic bins full of tiny parts.** It's fun running your hand through hundreds of drywall screw holders, rubber tap seals, or those plastic things you sometimes see in bricks.

As you walk down those creaking wooden floors, through **dusty sunbeam rays** shining over dirty floor mats, don't forget to let that jingle-jangly door clang shut on your Saturday-morning sniff down memory lane.

AWESOME!

Putting on your most flattering pair of pants

Just slide smoothly into that second skin and get ready to rock the streets with your **perfectly wrapped package**. Yes, it's time to shake that booty and get ready to look great, girlfriend.

Suddenly chubby legs get the trim-down treatment, **saggy flabs get toned**, and all the dark creases crinkle in just the right places and just the right spaces.

See, we all have that **one perfect pair** of pants that fits us best. And we all know how it feels throwing them on before heading out.

AWESOME!

That guy who helps you parallel park

....

I suck at parallel parking.

Honestly, just look at me out there: tyre-scraping, **curb-bumping**, seven-point turning in the middle of the busy street. Yes, that's why I always breathe a **massive sigh of relief** when someone stops by to lend me a hand:

1. **Airport Crew Chief.** Strap a neon vest and giant ear-muffs on this gal because she's straight off the land-ing strip. If you're lucky she'll stand in your side mirror and use that beautiful two-hands-getting-closer-together technique.

2. **The Extremist.** Dude's an extreme screamer with no middle ground. Some of his favourite lines are: "Back back back back back ba— STOP!," "Whoa. Whoa! WhoawhoawhoaWHOAWHOOOAH!," and "Lots of space lots of space lots of—you're on the curb."

3. **Mr Measures.** This guy's straight outta the classroom and all about the accuracy. He'll be dusting chalk

off his hands while inspecting your bumper and
calling out, "You've still got four centimetres."

We sure do love these kind footpath souls. Without their
help we'd be craning our necks and **twisting our spines** so it's
great when they pop on by to help us pop on in.
AWESOME!

Peeling your socks off under the sheets

....

Skip the shock.

People, we all know how bad your feet have it. They've been through a lot today so no need nailing them with a blast of cold air before bed. Instead, just tuck them in tightly, **tuck them in rightly**, and peel off your socks using only your feet when you're warm and comfy under the sheets.

Don't worry—you can collect the **sweaty sock mounds** from the foot of your bed tomorrow.

Sweet dreams.

AWESOME!

Napping with somebody else

Jam your elbows in that stomach, breathe in those **shampoo fumes**, and squeeze your knees into the puffy cushions while spooning into a quick catnap on the couch. As drool drips, skin warms, and a **slippery sweatfilm** slides between you, just smile, close your eyes, and fade into a quiet cuddly moment with someone you love.

AWESOME!

Getting a stuck ball out of somewhere by using another ball

....

This is the childhood version of Mr Fixit.

Whether you're shooting free throws in the driveway, **whipping tennis balls at a wall**, or tossing Frisbees in the park, it always happens, man. Someone tosses it a bit too high or a bit too wobbly and suddenly your whole game gets stuck in a tight squeeze. Now the basketball is behind the backboard, the tennis ball is on the roof, and the Frisbee is stuck in the tree.

Of course the best way to get that ball out is by using its family members against it. This is the backyard equivalent of putting the **hostage taker's mum** on the phone during the tense negotiations.

"Antonio, please. It's your mother. You don't have to do this," the bald, withered tennis ball in the crowded street pleads over the radio to the scarred one sitting in the gutter.

"I love you, Antonio."

Using one ball to rescue another is always effective as long as you watch out for these potential trip-ups along the way:

1. **Double Down.** This is when your second ball joins the first ball instead of popping it out. Now you've got mum and son in the gutter and you're running out of things to toss. Bring out the ladder, hockey stick, or swimming pool noodles.

2. **It's Raining Running Shoes.** This is the opposite of the double down. In this case the good news is the tennis racquet, garden stones, or running shoes you tossed up there did the job. The bad news is you weren't ready for both to fall so you took a hard Reebok to the kisser.

3. **The Understudy.** You popped the wedged basketball out, but the other ball you threw up there got stuck behind the backboard. If you listen you'll hear as a voice announces on the PA system too. "Ladies and gentlemen, your attention please. The role of tightly wedged Spalding in tonight's performance will be played by half-deflated volleyball."

4. **The Sunset.** This is where you take so long to dislodge the football out of the tree that the sun sets and forces you to come back tomorrow. The Sunset can also happen when you're the one who got the ball stuck to begin with so your friends wait till you pass it down before leaving you up there to enjoy the view.

Now, let's not let those **trip-ups** cool down our buzz, because we all know another ball generally does the job just fine. Good luck, driveway warriors.

AWESOME!

Seeing a number plate from home when you're somewhere really far away

Every plate has a story.

Maybe it's a **cab of uni students** on an endless summer road trip. Beef jerky wrappers, stained T-shirts, and a sweaty cooler fill the backseat of the rusty Volvo as they cruise cross-country to soak in some **sunny freedom** before school starts. You see them laughing in front of you with a plate from your hometown and you smile softly at distant days gone by . . .

Or maybe it's a couple of retirees from the same state as you out enjoying the first few weeks of a brand new life. As you pass their **big boxy RV** in the slow lane, you peek in and notice a wrinkly driver in a tight baseball cap and **baggy pink shirt** steering fiercely with a big twinkle in her eye. Your brain backflips as you daydream about your last day of work . . .

Or maybe it's a family station wagon filling up at the pumps with a canoe on the roof and sleeping bags in the window. They're heading up north the same way you are and inside two kids play video games in **crumbs and juice stains** as baby chews Cheerios and falls fast asleep. You glance at your boyfriend riding shotgun and he looks up innocently and smiles . . .

Yes, seeing a number plate from your home in a place far, far away is just a little winking reminder that we're all joined from the edge of our driveway to the edge of your driveway. Dusty towns, big cities, **open fields**, and tree-lined lanes may lie between us . . . but the truth is we're all in this together: bouncing in cars, **swerving down roads**, spinning in place, flying through space.

AWESOME!

The moment on holiday when you forget what day of the week it is

....

Let's see here.

Saturday we got here. Sunday we did nothing. Then after that we did nothing. The next day we did nothing. And we're doing nothing now.

AWESOME!

Hanging out with your mum

My mum and I saw a movie the other night.

I zoomed up the highway from my CBD apartment and she got a lift through the **quiet side streets** of my hometown. She had a big smile when I got there and was waiting in the lobby wearing lipstick and a **cream cable-knit jumper**. She had the tickets prepurchased and a handbag packed with white chocolate, **mixed nuts**, and two bottles of water.

A plump n' perky assistant manager with curls waterfalling out of her tight baseball cap ripped our tickets and pointed us down the hall. We passed a couple of **glossy-eyed teens** holding mops and had a quick discussion—Where do you want to sit? Where do *you* want to sit? Wherever you want to sit—before grabbing a couple in the middle of the **red plushy tundra**.

Now, my mum's **five feet tall** so her legs dangled from the chair, her clean grey **spongy-soled sneakers** swaying like a kid on a swing set. We chatted, chilled, and chowed down on chocolate before leaning back for the start of the show.

My mum fell asleep in twenty minutes.

I elbowed her softly and her eyes popped open. She looked at me, **laughed guiltily**, and whispered in a mock-cranky tone, "It's past my bedtime!" She then watched for a few more minutes before dozing off again. After a couple more elbow jabs, I eventually just let her go.

When the credits started rolling and the houselights turned up we put on our coats and made our way down. "So what did you think of the ending?" I asked with a big smile. "I liked the way they wrapped things up," she straight-faced back, holding the **metal handrail** and single-stepping down the stairs.

I drove her home down the quiet, **wet-slicked roads**, through empty intersections, past my old school and the park where my sister and I had soccer practice. When we reached the house, she smiled groggily, **gave me a big hug**, and said come back soon.

As I zipped down the highway into the **bright city lights** my brain photo-flashed back . . . to blurry images of late-night rides through those same empty intersections, photos flashing from **front-row seats at school plays**, and cold wobbly lawn chairs sitting patiently for hours on the sidelines of rainy soccer practices . . .

AWESOME!

When the person you're meeting is even later than you are

....

Crap, crap, crap, crap, crap.

You're late.

Racing, **running**, rushing, you're checking your watch and picturing your friend **tapping their foot** and rolling their eyes while waiting for you.

That's why it's great when you arrive hot, **sweaty,** and breathless just before they rush around the corner hot, sweaty, and breathless too.

Now no one has to feel bad.

AWESOME!

Riding your bike really late at night when the streets are completely empty

....

Now's your time.

As the sun dips down and the twilight fades to darkness there's nothing sweeter than wheeling your bike out of the garage for a late summer night cruise. Those freewheeling adventures are great for a few reasons:

- **The sound of silence.** Hello darkness, my old friend. I've come to ride with you again. Yes, blaring horns, squealing brakes, and revving engines are all turned down and you're left alone in the shadows with the wind whispering in your ears.
- **Danger, Will Robinson.** There's a sense of reckless cool cruising down those lonely black roads. You can swerve your bike in all directions, hop off the curbs, and be a two-wheeled free spirit.
- **Street King.** House lights flick off and raccoons paw rubbish bins as you rule your Neighbourhood Empire as the newly crowned Street King. Puff your chest and scream, "Get off my land!" at passing

motorists. Just keep that crown under your helmet for safety.

Yes, riding your bike late at night lets you be alone with your thoughts and your dreams and your fears all **rolling around your brain** as you roll around the block. Chatty parents, **buzzing phones**, and little brothers are all left behind as you stare forward into the blackness and ride on and on and on . . .

AWESOME!

Dropping your mobile phone on the footpath and then realising it's totally fine

It's a terrible scene.

As that mobile phone, digital camera, or pair of sunglasses **crash-lands on the concrete,** everyone gasps as it crunches, bounces, and skids hard . . .

Suddenly your eyes blur, **stomach twists,** and world flips as you fade back and realise you're somehow **covered in scrubs** inside a busy hospital ER.

You glance down the hall and see **ambulance guys** racing toward you wheeling your bloody mobile phone strapped to a gurney without any noticeable lights or beeps. Someone's got an icebox holding the battery case that blew off and a nurse is screaming that **signal strength** has flatlined.

Your eyebrows furrow and pupils dilate as you snap on latex gloves, **pull up your surgical mask,** and start frantically checking for vitals. You scan for signs of blunt trauma, pop the battery in and out, and then finally stare straight into your mobile phone's face while **closing your eyes,** wincing, and forcing yourself to push Power.

There is a pause.

Nurses lean in with wide, hopeful eyes, ambulance guys jostle and crowd, and **nervous friends** squeeze their own phones tightly for comfort and support. Then suddenly as everyone waits . . . and waits . . . and waits . . .

The power flashes and blinks back on.

And there is cheering.

AWESOME!

Discovering a shortcut on your way home

Move over, Marco Polo.

Columbus, Clark, and Cortes, you got nothing, either.

Sure, maybe you sailed over choppy waves, **fought with cannibals**, and documented distant lands. Maybe you traded silk with kings, **discovered precious stones**, and toppled terrible empires. Maybe you even found new technologies and trade routes while helping us realise the Earth wasn't flat.

But we just figured out cutting through the chemist's car park saves us ten seconds.

Beat that.

AWESOME!

Finally realising where you know someone from after staring at them forever

··

We're all bad at names but sometimes faces stick in our brains.

Yes, when you see **Familiar Brown-Haired Man** walk by the bus stop or **Curly Redhead Lady** eating fries in the food court you suddenly do a double take and think, "Wait . . . I know them from somewhere."

That's when you stop chewing your gum, **stop talking to your friends**, and stop sending blood to nonvital organs. All the tiny men in your head wake up, put on their boots, and fire-pole down to your brain's dusty archives. Suddenly they're fishing through files, **scanning databases**, and booting up old hard drives to comb every neuron you've got for trace clues of who you're staring at.

Photos flash of high school dances, **first jobs**, and uni parties. You imagine beards and moustaches, picture them in baseball caps, or mentally dye their hair blond. Your mind reels through old friends' girlfriends, people who owe you money, and cousins from the other side of the family you met at a distant wedding.

Or maybe you don't recognise them for a while simply because **they're out of context**. It's your phys ed teacher squeezing melons at the supermarket, your barber jogging in a jumpsuit at the park, or the office assistant from your old job sweating buckets on the treadmill.

Sometimes it seems like they're looking at you the exact same way too. You wonder if their **little brain men** are combing through databases or if they recognise you but just aren't saying anything. You wonder and wonder and **think and think** and stare and stare until!

It clicks.

And that's a beautiful moment of sweet relief. The little brain men slam **filing cabinets** and cheer, one of them pulls the steam whistle and smoke flies out your ears, and a slow and satisfied smile curls onto your face as you finally place the mystery person.

Then maybe you say hi or something.

AWESOME!

When the houseguest leaves

You're here!!!

Come in, **come in**, come in, make yourself at home, make yourself at home. Here, let me get your coat and I'll throw your bag upstairs. Go ahead, grab a drink, have a seat, I'll be right back.

Okay, so! How are you! It's so good to see you! Relax, sit down . . . what can I get you? Are you hungry, thirsty? Do you want a Coke, orange juice, water? Just water? Alright, with or without ice? Are you sure you're not hungry? Want like a grilled cheese or something? **Oh, wait!** I've got leftover lasagna from last night. Do you want some? No, no, I can't eat it all anyway. Don't worry about it. I'll just heat up a piece, no problem. It'll just be a second. Have a seat! Sit down, sit down, relax, you drove a long way. Relax!

So . . . what time do you usually get up? Me, I'm around 8:30. Oh . . . no, no, no, that's fine. I'll just get up a bit earlier so you can jump in right after me. No, it's no problem. I left some towels on your bed and there's a hair dryer under the sink. Do you need an alarm clock? Oh, what do you like for breakfast? Yeah, yeah, I've got cereal. Actually, you know what, we need milk. I'm just going to pop to the corner and grab some real quick so we're good for morning. **No, it's no**

problem! You can use my computer if you want to check your email before going to bed. I know you're tired. Goodnight! Sleep tight!

Morning!!! Did you sleep well? Oh . . . sorry, I should have told you there were extra blankets in the closet. No, don't worry about making the bed, I'll wash the sheets tonight when I get home. I'm so glad you came over, honestly. It was great catching up. It's been forever.

Alright, have a great day. Take care, let's talk soon. Thanks again for coming over!

Bye!!!!!!!!!!

AWESOME!

Placing the last piece of the puzzle

I don't have the patience for puzzles.

If someone walks into the room shaking a big **500-piece box** with a photo of a grey boulder balanced **on a grey cliff**, then I'm not having it.

Okay, I might help you find the **corner pieces** or start the first edge, but that's it. After it gets into the **no-man's-land** of middle pieces, and people start making stack-piles of colours, passing around the box top and squinting, and silently trying to clip piece after piece after piece together, well, I just can't take it anymore.

When everybody crowds around the coffee table, I start sulking and retreat to the couch where I occupy myself with productive jobs such as **piling all the coasters**, finger-dragging the crumbs out the side of the cushions, or trying to eat a potato chip without chewing it, which is actually much more difficult than it sounds.

This is why it's so great when someone finally places the last piece of the puzzle.

There's usually giddy anticipation as the pace quickens toward the finale. All fingers get into the game, attaching the two giant puzzle chunks together, and then someone finally drops in **that one piece** we all knew was here somewhere with the other half of the **bird's wing** on it.

Hey, the last piece of the puzzle is great because it means **you have the last piece of the puzzle.** Let's not overlook this fact. After all, who among us hasn't picked up a cheapo garage sale special only to discover it was four pieces short when you were putting it together? Talk about a buzz kill.

Secondly, it means you finally get to see the big picture. Up until that point it's all poking, prodding, and passing around the dog-eared box top, but now we've got a poster. Some people mount these things and stick them on a wall. Nothing wrong with that.

Lastly, there is a thick and heady sense of **smoking satisfaction** in the air. Even though I'm probably spilling a tall glass of wine and flipping past infomercials at this point, even I can feel it. The gang all pitched in, helped out, and accomplished the big mission together.

Now the party can really get nuts.

AWESOME!

When you know someone well enough to go in their fridge without asking

Talk about an intimate moment.

It's one thing to strike up a conversation, **grab drinks after work,** start hanging on weekends, and become close friends.

It's another thing to have open fridge access.

Honestly, if you're cool with **sharing your food supply,** then you two are tight like twins. You've probably known each other so long that all **courtesies have gone** out the window in favour of **getting cozy** on the couch with some juice and puddings.

When someone grabs a bunch of grapes from your crisper, snags cold pizza from the box, or starts making a sandwich with whatever's around, then I've got news for you.

You've got yourself a best friend.

AWESOME!

When you finish your milkshake and then remember there's more in that stainless steel cup

How delicious was that thick and creamy shake you just slurped through the fat straw at the roadside cafe? Sitting in the torn vinyl booths by the jukebox, you drank those tiny bubbles, **slurped cold clumps**, and shot back all the swirling sweet cream at the bottom of the glass.

Your entire body shivered and shook and you sucked back that delicious frosty glass of milkshake.

And guess what?

There's more.

AWESOME!

Emptying the recycling bin on your computer

As old school assignments, **half-downloaded MP3s**, and duplicate photos crumple and disappear from your hard drive, you settle back into your office chair, slap your hands together, and smile at finishing up The World's Easiest Chore.

AWESOME!

Waking up to the smell of sizzling bacon

Lazing around in crumpled sheets, sun streaking through the blinds, you open your eyes and blink slowly while your lips curl into a smile. You glance casually at the alarm clock, stare at the ceiling, and flip your pillow.

Then it hits you.

Nose twitching, brain sniffing, you catch **faint fumes** of something sizzling in the kitchen. Can it be? Is this why you woke up? You bunny-sniff again and this time you're positive, you're certain, you're sure.

Bacon!!!

It smells like mum's cooking breakfast on a holiday morning. It smells like a sunny Sunday at the **chilly campsite** with your boyfriend. It smells like pyjamas and a fresh newspaper with your uni flatmates.

It smells like little white grease bubbles in a crispy black pan.

And it smells a lot like

AWESOME!

Jumping as many stairs as possible

....

Racing up staircases or jumping down them gives you that **I'm-in-a-rush** rush. Handrails play helper as you leap on stage as the quick-zipping star of the show. Let's chat about how to make the magic happen.

Okay, if you're going **up**, two of the classiest moves include:

1. **Roboto Man**. You're a straight-faced, mild-mannered Stairskipper 4000, an advanced prototype who skips steps nonchalantly and even does the triple step every so often. Robotos sometimes act super casual because they're quietly racing someone in the escalator beside them.

2. **Eager Beavers**. These are sweaty six-year-olds who just scoffed all their lollies, businesswomen racing to catch the commuter train, or teenagers in baseball caps and baseball gloves running to the park. Eager beavers sometimes leap up two, three, four stairs at a time. Although it's in their best interest

to avoid you, keep your eyes peeled for sharp elbows and sweat showers.

Okay, if you're going **down** I recommend one of the following:

1. **The Tarzan**. Some lords of the jungle motor down the stairs and then plant their hands on the rail to swing themselves the rest of the way. We've all heard long tales of six, seven, even eight steps at once, but details are always fuzzy and hard to confirm. Still, if done well The Tarzan can be majestic. If done poorly, it can be ankle sprainy.
2. **Cliff Jumpers**. This one's for pros only. This is just a huge, free-falling jump, generally on the way down to the basement to play video games. Hopefully you've got a padded cushion landing and don't crash through the wood veneer wall. There is no limit to the heights you can reach with this move.

Jumping as many stairs as possible gets your blood flowing from **mini cardio workouts** throughout the day. For a few brief moments you transform from a gal on her way to biology class into an animal in the wild again—scaling mountains, skipping rivers, leaping off cliffs like you were born to do. Your ancestors did the dirty work for hundreds of thousands of years, so make sure you pay honour to your **primal roots** and caveman instincts whenever you jump some stairs.

Jump up.

Jump down.

Jump forever.

AWESOME!

Screaming at characters in movies to do things

"No!"

"Don't, don't, don't."

"Don't, he's behind the door."

"Turn around!"

"Turn around, turn around, turn around!"

"Now kiss her, you idiot."

AWESOME!

When your friends working in fast-food restaurants give you a little extra

....

Sure, sure, we're all honest people here.

You and me, we're driving the speed limit, **crossing at crossings**, and never double parking. But that doesn't mean we don't like bonus fries, extra-scoopy ice cream, or double cheese on our subs.

Hey, when that gal behind the smooth orange counter wearing the paper hat and **pin-striped shirt** is your pal from high school, it's time for a little extra whipped cream and chocolate sauce on that drippy ice cream sundae.

It's just the Fast-Food Workers' Pact.

AWESOME!

Wearing what you just bought out of the shop

Sometimes those old, ratty sandals need to get buried. When footpath steps rattle your spine and walking to the shop gives you **severe blackfoot**, it's time to go shopping.

Next time you slide on that fresh new pair in the shop, just pause for a second and look wistfully at the broken, smooth-soled flat ones in your hand. So many rainy nights, so many deck parties, so many quick trips for petrol. Fight tears and **steady your lip** as you stare the teenage cashier square in the eye and say:

"Do you guys have a rubbish bin?"

AWESOME!

Finally peeing after holding it forever

··

It didn't used to be this way.

For hundreds of thousands of years our species peed freely, **whenever**, wherever. Yes, whether we were roaming jungles, **crossing ice bridges**, or having picnics in plains, it wasn't always pretty but when nature called, we answered.

Sadly, things are different now.

Most of the time our bladders are all locked up.

With our stadium seating, **boardroom meetings**, kids' soccer games, and smooth highway lanes, the one thing we didn't build in was an easy way to clear some leaves and **squat in the corner**. Honestly, how many times have you been looking for parking and circling the car park, waiting for a movie to wrap up the plot, or just fumbling with keys so you could race to the pot?

Listen, I've been there too. Yes, it's always a tight squeeze, **with bouncing knees** and gritted teeth, but we accept this trade-off in exchange for living in our bright and modern **World of Pants**. And a world where everybody wears pants is great, don't get me wrong. It's just that it cramps our style sometimes.

That's why finally peeing after holding it forever feels so great. It's like millions of years of **animalistic need** bursting through the chains and restraints of modern social norms. It's the bathroom equivalent of a **primal scream** and it feels oh so incredibly

AWESOME!

The night before a really big day

....

Stare at that ceiling.

Sweaty palms, **white knuckles**, deep breaths in bed.

Maybe the ring's stowed away and **the reservations are made.** Maybe the results are coming in and everyone's coming over. Maybe you're buttoning down for a new job or **following your heart** and leaving an old one.

Moonlight shines in your window as excitement bubbles in your brain.

It's almost here.

AWESOME!

Finding the perfect patch of grass to sit on at the park

Here's how to find that magic grass:

1. **Dampness Double Check**. Nobody likes a wet bottom. Keep your backside dry by spying classic signs like slightly dipped areas or permanently shady patches. May also be worth tapping the ground to check with your hand or do a five-second Practice Sit, which involves sitting down and staring straight ahead while activating the cold, wet sensors in your track pants.

2. **Sticks and Stones**. They may break your bones, but more important they're no fun to sit on. Plus, they're a dangerous omen of protruding tree roots, prickly weeds, and grassless patches of hard dirt. Stay away.

3. **Temp Check**. On hot days you're looking for shady patches under tall trees, on cool days you're scoping sunny spots by the sandpit, and sometimes you can't decide so you search for that perfect square of half-and-half.

4. **Frisbee Lookout**. Some parks have a lot of activities going on. Shaggy-haired dudes in hemp necklaces and bare feet toss Frisbees, dads play catch with their kids, and tiny toddlers in T-shirts and nappies run around playing Chase The Dog or Run Till You Faceplant. If you're looking to relax, you've got to avoid this happy chaos.

Sometimes those sunny Saturday afternoons are just begging for a casual walk to your local park. Grab a coffee, throw the kids in a stroller, or walk a dog with friends. As that breeze blows by just close your eyes and enjoy a few quiet minutes of relaxing and soaking it all in.

AWESOME!

When you hit the point where you're comfortable farting around each other

....

I fart, **you fart**, he farts, she farts.

Let's not deny it, people. Farting is a regular, healthy, and hilarious part of life. Squeezing out big plumes of noxious gas doesn't always smell good, but it generally feels mighty fine.

Now think back for a second to the last time you heard a tiny baby pop out a **stinky heater**. I'm betting after they filled the air they just stared at you with a blank expression that seemed to say, "Yeah, it was me. So what?"

And maybe that's a good thing.

Maybe when your boyfriend's snuggling with you under the blanket and there's a few chirps from the back of his pants, **that's good**. Maybe when Grandpa leans back on his rocker and lets one rip during Sunday dinner, **that's good**. Maybe when your wife nonchalantly blasts one while barbecuing on the balcony, **that's good**.

And maybe it's especially good when everyone laughs afterward.

Because hey, it just means we're comfortable being ourselves and relaxed enough to know farting is a natural and normal part of life. Nobody chooses farting as a hobby but it's part of what makes us human. Tuba scales, **silent stink bombs**, machine-gun blasts, whatever you're putting out there, that's fine, that's fine, that's perfectly fine.

Now, we're not advocating a world of **no limits**. There's nothing wrong with keeping some personal space either. After all, maybe you do your nose picking in the car, shower behind a curtain at the gym, or burp quietly into a fancy cloth napkin. If so, that's cool too.

All we're saying is that if you get to the point where you're comfortable farting around each other, it means you're family, you're friends, or you're **completely in love**.

So just relax and let it out.

AWESOME!

Walking into class and seeing a substitute teacher

Postpone the pop quiz, **lose the science lab**, axe the algebra lesson.

Now's the time when **energy bolts** blast through brains as everybody revs up for forty-five minutes of whispering, **passing notes**, and tossing paper aeroplanes.

AWESOME!

Fully justifying whatever terrible thing you're eating

Let the grease glisten, **mayo drip**, and soft drink fizz.

Here are three ways to make the magic happen:

1. **Veggie Validation.** My friend Mike is king of this move. "Gotta get my greens," he'll say, while chomping dill pickles on the couch playing video games. "Carrots are good for you," he'll smirk, while licking thick cream cheese icing off a moist brick of carrot cake. Remember: Anything with vegetables in it fully qualifies as potentially healthy. Now go relax and enjoy a slice of pumpkin pie with a side of onion rings.

2. **Dumbbell Defence.** On the rare mornings I venture to the gym for a half-dozen sit-ups and some stretching in track pants, I always end up eating a tipsy mountain of nachos for dinner later in the day. "No worries," I'll think with cheese-greasy fingers and salsa dripping down my chin. "I totally worked this off already."

3. **Holiday Breakin'.** When you go on holidays it's fun to free your stomach from the shackles of the

kitchen. Slip into shades and shorts and start breaking the rules in the slow lane. Remember: Getting away from it all means putting your feet up and having a third sundae.

Yes, fully justifying whatever terrible thing you're eating is a beautiful eyes-wide moment of taste-based wonder. It's great ditching the guilt once in a while to enjoy a **crispy-skinned frankfurt** on the footpath or a drippy Quarter Pounder after the bars on Friday night.

People, we ain't **spinning on this rock** too long, so let's all remember to relax and just enjoy the extra scoop.

AWESOME!

When you get the scissors at that perfect angle where it slices through wrapping paper with no effort from you

....

I'm a terrible gift wrapper.

Yes, I'm the guy who cuts off too much paper, **overtapes the ends**, and realises when I think I'm done that the corner of the present is still visible so I've got to add random patches of paper from rogue scraps off the floor.

I'm a sharp-n-sticky, **tape-n-scissors disaster** sitting in a hunched-over clump on the family room carpet with squashed bows and twisted ribbons scattered all around me.

Honestly, the only time I'm on top of my game is when I manage to snip my scissors into the paper at **that perfect angle** where it just glides across the sheet in one beautiful sweeping slice.

That's when I suddenly ditch my incompetence for a beautifully brief moment of gift-wrapping

AWESOME!

Becoming a regular somewhere

....

Come on in.

We all know that being a regular doesn't just happen overnight. No, it's more like softly falling into a slow romance with a new friend . . .

> **Stage 1: The First Glance.** There are plenty of fish in the sea and they're all eager for your attention, but you slowly pick one out. Maybe it's the big coffee cups, the wrinkly newspapers on the counter, or the late night hours that keep it open when you can't sleep. Something made this coffee shop stand out and you felt at home right away.

> **Stage 2: They Like You Too.** Slowly your favourite spot gets more and more of your time. You were a bit of a coffee shop tramp before this, dashing through drive-thrus and grabbing quickies from the vending machine in the cafeteria. But without realising it, you've started giving this new place your time . . . and they noticed. One day you see the server crack a little smile when

you walk in and give a quick nod before you place your order.

Stage 3: The First Date. Suddenly the cold market forces warm into a little cloud of human connection. It's the same guy behind the counter but now there's recognition and an opening line. Maybe "Did you like the extra nutmeg in your cappuccino yesterday?" or "Blueberry scone, extra butter, right?" or "I think I saw you playing downtown yesterday. Brian, was it?" When your coffee shop puts itself out there, make sure you accept it with open arms. "That's what it was? Delicious!" "Yeah, not that I need it!" or "Oh cool, do you hang out there often?" will do.

Stage 4: The Courtship. Now you start smiling and taking care of each other. You've got exact change ready to go, the server's got your cappuccino with extra nutmeg. Head nods replace verbal orders and you smirk and smile together at other customers, kind of like you're behind the counter too. There's some nervous anticipation when you walk in the door: Who will be working the espresso machine this morning? Will they still have the Sports section? Will the biscuits be warm?

Stage 5: The Living Together. You fall into a warm and cozy comfort that's beyond words. Hellos and how-are-yous fade into chats about whether you should get a dog or advice on dealing with a new boss. You get your order your way, right away, every time, and sometimes even skip the line. You start sharing tables and newspapers with other regulars and making little jokes with them like "Oh, you always beat me on Saturdays!" You're now in the cozy zone of the inner circle. Welcome to paradise.

Stage 6: The Almost-Break-up. The change happens quick and it jars you senseless. Maybe your favourite cashier moves away for school or the shop closes for three weeks for major renovations. The shock hits you hard but you resolve to get through it. Maybe you decide this is just what you needed to keep things fresh, so you dig deep and change yourself. Suddenly you're getting black coffee instead of lattes, getting to know the new cashier, and loving those new paper towel dispensers in the bathroom.

Stage 7: The Future. Time moves by and things change but your souls remain connected. Sometimes you think about the past: Remember when they got new chairs? Or the time the power went out and they gave away cake? You've been through so much together that **you've actually become** part of the place. You helped set up their Internet, fixed the wobbly table, and co-invented the chocolate chip peanut butter biscuit.

In these anonymous days of big-box shops, gated communities, and rampant Interneting, there's something special about becoming a regular and feeling human connection in your human heart. When you visit your favourite joint it's like welcome back to your corner stool, welcome back to your favourite table, welcome back to your perfect order.

Welcome back to being a regular.

Welcome back to love.

AWESOME!

When a friend starts randomly giving you a massage

There's a few magic ways this deed goes down:

1. **The Couch Classic.** Snuggling up under the blankets, you're warm and cozy in a dark basement in front of a flickering screen. It's late, it's quiet, and suddenly your sister or boyfriend behind you starts softly rubbing your neck and shoulders. All the aches in the world disappear into the abyss as you sigh softly and melt deeper and deeper into the comfy confines of the couch.

2. **The Scalper.** This one's a bit rare since it requires sitting in a chair in front of somebody standing up. But occasionally that's exactly the scene when that somebody starts randomly rubbing your head. Now your achy breaky brain is loving the head circulation from that ten-finger rubdown.

3. **The Foot Surprise.** Some people say feet are disgusting. These people are not me. No, I say feet are our body's most loyal soldiers who take a beating and deserve to be treated right. Unfortunately, it's tricky massaging your own feet, and asking some-

one to do it can be a bit off-limits. ("Hey, Thompson, when you're done with that drywall, can I ask you a huge favour?") That's why it's so special when someone starts giving you a secret foot rub. Thanks for doing what we were all afraid to ask for.

Yes, you were just sitting there a **sore ball of knots** until you started getting a friendly massage and instantly melted into a soft blissed-out puddle of
AWESOME!

Walking around naked when you're home alone

You are charged with one count of checking yourself out in the mirror, two counts of **irresponsible couch usage**, four counts of shower-to-bedroom carpet drippage, and seventeen counts of temporary nudity of the first degree.

How do you plead?

AWESOME!

Anything on tap

Once upon a time my friend Chad went to university.

Now, Chad likes to tell people what made him decide to go to school and the reasons why he traded in a job at **Best Buy** for a few hard years of hitting the books.

See, on a whim one weekend Chad packed his boot and cruised down the highway to visit our friend Mike who was away at school. They didn't have any plans but spent a couple of days going out for drinks and eating meals at the residence dining hall.

And it was in that dining hall that Chad first came face-to-face with a big beautiful **stainless steel** object of his desire. Yes, he glanced up slowly and realised in a stunning moment that he was staring straight at **chocolate milk on tap.**

His jaw dropped and his eyeballs flashed fireworks as he immediately filled three glasses with the sweet-flowing **brown gold** and let his brain reel with infinite possibilities.

"It's like neverending chocolate milk," he started, his head bobbing in quick nods excitedly. And then a second later: "I gotta go to uni!"

This is actually a true story. Chocolate milk on tap convinced Chad to ditch his job and head down the highway the following year. Chocolate milk on tap changed his life because **anything on tap** is great. Let's count down some killer classics:

- **Slurpees.** Flip the switch sideways and let the crystal cola slide smoothly into your cup like a snake. For bonus points, mix and match flavours until your drink looks like the surface of Jupiter.
- **Brown soft drink aka Swamp Water.** Did you ever get behind an open bar at a wedding when you were a kid? If you remember mixing tall glasses of fountain Coke, Sprite, and cream soda into a delightfully tangy swill, then you had a great childhood.
- **Beer at a keg party**. Forget the bottles and cans for a night. Now it's time for some foamy pumping. If you're the one guy who actually knows how to tap the keg, then you're the official dude responsible for keeping everyone else's red plastic cup full.
- **Maple syrup.** Just toss on your hiking boots in the dead of winter, walk silently to the middle of the forest, and tap that tree to get it done, son. It's time to get sticky. (Note: May require hours of boiling.)
- **Soft-serve ice cream.** Don't you love it when your local buffet has a soft-serve ice cream machine sitting right in the open? You can squeeze a little

swirl into your warm, plastic wet-from-the-dish-washer bowl, or go cowboy and build the tallest, swirliest ice cream known to man.

- **Water.** If you've got a drink in the kitchen, clean hands in the bathroom, and a hot shower in the tub, then today's your day to say thanks.
- **Condiment pumps.** Pump that watery tomato sauce and watch out for unexpected mustard opportunities.
- **The hot chocolate machine** at a camp, cabin, or chalet. Let the good stuff pour out and let's curl by the fire in thick wool jumpers under big poofy blankets.
- **Nacho cheese at the corner shop.** Now, here's the heaviest hitter of all. When you swirl your salty nachos under that hot pump of oozing cheese, you're in for a good night.

Years later we were sitting around late one night and Chad once again told his famous chocolate milk story. Someone new piped in with a confused look and said, "So, Chad, did it actually change your life?" Chad responded right away. "Chocolate milk changed my life by confirming my desire to go to uni. Uni changed my life because I realised there was more to taps than chocolate. There was beer and cider. There was mustard at the hot dog trolley. There was instant water for hot chocolate, oatmeal, and tea. It really made me realise that this world has so many things to offer, on tap."

So let's all say it here today: When we come face-to-face with **anything on tap,** all cans and bottles fade to black. We'll just grab control of the boat and start pumping nozzles and **squeezing triggers** with reckless abandon, breaking free of the tight shackles of portion control and sailing deeper and deeper into a shadowy paradise of no rules . . . no order . . . and no limits.

AWESOME!

When you sneeze and a stranger says bless you

Warm Sunday dinners with family, late nights drinking with friends, studying with a group in your basement.

All of these are **high-odds scenes** for scoring a blessing after you sneeze. Chances are good that if you explode in a loud bang of spit and phlegm at the dinner table, at least one of your aunts will say "Bless you" and there's a good shot everyone will chime in. Same when you're grabbing wings or cramming for biology.

But when you're on your own, it's a whole different story.

Tapping on a laptop at the library, washing your hands in the restaurant bathroom, double-stepping up the escalator on your way to work.

These are **low-odds scenes** for netting a blessing. The people around you don't know you and maybe don't notice you. But when you sneeze and there's just silence, it's a bit awkward. I always feel a little lonely in those situations. "Didn't anyone just hear me sneeze?" I want to ask. But instead I just finish washing my hands and wonder if my released spirit is now floating around the urinals.

This is why there's something cool about a stranger saying bless you. It's even better when you say nothing before the free blessing and they say nothing afterward. Like a friendly smile on a passing escalator or an empathetic laugh behind you in line, it's just a momentary little **politeness blip**.

AWESOME!

Rubbing someone's newly shaved head

Feel the buzz and rub that fuzz.

AWESOME!

Looking at how much dirt came off something you just cleaned

My apartment looks over a busy CBD intersection.

Shredded bird feathers, **swirling dust funnels**, and car exhaust fumes cover my balcony in a thick layer of city grime.

If you come over and go out there, I'll tell you to put shoes on or suffer **shocking sockicide**. Don't believe me and your white socks will suffer a case of career-ending blackfoot. It's a bad way to go and generally results in grabbing a new pair on the way home.

The worst part isn't the balcony floor, though. **It's the table and chairs.** They get slimed too but are harder to cover up. I can't just say, "Oh, before you sit down, grab a plastic bag from under the sink and tuck it into your jeans. Thanks!"

No, I can't do that, I won't do that, **I don't do that**. Instead, I grab a hunk of wet paper towels and slide them all over the chairs and tables while my guests watch with jaw-dropping disgust. The thick mat quickly turns the **blackest black** you've ever seen and I sort of smile and wave it in their face before going inside to throw it out.

And . . . you know why I smile? You know why I wave it in their face? Besides the fact that I'm not a very nice person,

I mean. Well, I'll tell you why: because **I'm proud** of how much dirt came off. To me it's a sense of accomplishment. It's the same as showing your sister that floor cloth with every **square molecule** covered in dust and cat hair. It's the awe with which you stare at the McDonald's serviette that just swabbed all that wet, yellowy grease off your forehead. It's the sensation of looking at the disgustingly dirty tissue after wiping down your TV screen for the first time in a year.

Looking at how much dirt came off something you just cleaned causes some big swelling feelings to swish together inside you. It's accomplishment, it's cleanliness, and most of all it's "I'm glad I'm not sitting in that."

AWESOME!

Changing the channel during a commercial break and then flipping back just as the show's coming back on

It's even better if you accomplished something small while the commercials were running, like making some cheese and crackers, **throwing laundry in the dryer**, or putting the kids to bed.

You played a risky game, friend.

But you made it.

AWESOME!

When you meet up with a group of friends and they stop talking to celebrate your arrival

....

Sometimes you're late for the date.

Stepping into the dark restaurant, shaking off your umbrella, squeezing past the bar, you don't know what you're gonna get: Who's gonna be here? Have they already ordered? Will there even be a chair?

If you're like me, baby butterflies flutter in your stomach when you stumble into **Tonight's Social Scene** for the first time. Brushing rain off your eyebrows, unzipping your jacket, you smile nervously as you spot your friends and walk over to their crowded table in the back.

And if your entrance is marked by heads turning, forks dropping, fists raising, and loud cheers, it means you're hanging with a great group. So smile and accept their little **Welcome Package** of hugs and high fives.

It's gonna be a great night.

AWESOME!

Typing in your username and password at the speed of light

Put your hand up if you type slow.

Yes, if you're a clickity-clackity finger-punching purist whose **chubby fingers** stab at the keyboard with the rhythm and grace of a tiny bird picking pebbles at the park, then you're not alone.

Stumbling over emails, bumbling over book reports, you touch-type with a finger-bouncing pace that backspaces a bunch, slows down in a crunch, and gets twisted and snarled on big-word speed bumps.

Thank goodness you've got your **username and password** for some speed-of-lightning superfast quick typing.

Yes, when you log on to your computer or email account, your fingers suddenly take on a life of their own. They become possessed and you barely recognise them as they zip-zoom across the keys in a windy blur like **The Flash.**

Sometimes you really don't even know your password because your brain has **outsourced all memory** of it to your fingers which somehow always manage to come up with it right when you need it most.

AWESOME!

Finding hidden compartments in things you already own

My friend Rob welcomes visitors to his swanky apartment by flash-bulbing them in the face with a dusty old Polaroid camera.

After the picture slides out and the **colour fades in** he staples it to a foam board in his front hallway. Over time he's created a giant collage presumably titled **"Anybody Who's Ever Visited Me"** and turned a blank white wall into an artsy conversation piece.

When some friends and I crashed with Rob a year ago, he promptly **flash-bulbed us in the face** a couple of times. He handed me the extra pic while sticking the first on the wall and I stuffed it in my bags and forgot about it . . . forgot about it, that is, until months later I noticed a tiny white corner sticking out of my suitcase and rediscovered the blurry photo inside a **brand new secret pocket!**

Finding hidden compartments in things you already own is like striking oil in your own backyard.

After all, you've known your old pal **Backpack** forever. You know her zip's gummed up and you've watched with teary eyes as her stitching slowly ripped off her left strap. So when you notice a secret built-in pencil case pouch deep down in her inner shadows, it's a mind-blowing moment. Suddenly she's got a whole new strut in her step and trot in her walk, like she popped back out of backpack rehab.

Same thing with **Bathing Suit**. Sure, his zip-string is loose and dangly, he's covered in lint balls, and his bright red logo has faded to a dull pink, but when you first notice that tiny mesh pocket for holding keys hanging inside his elastic waistband, your brain blasts to outer space. He's like a hunched-over old man suddenly tossing away his cane and tap-dancing across the footpath.

So today let's give thanks and give cheers to the surprise sunglasses holder in the roof of your car, that second pocket in your navy blue blazer, and the **hidden change holder** riding like a treasure chest deep down in your car's armrest.

AWESOME!

Getting your guests to help you move something really heavy

....

Hey, thanks for coming over. Wait, wait, wait, hold on, uh, don't take off **your shoes** for a second. Listen, I've got this desk, and I sorta really need to get it out to the garage. Could you, I mean, it'll only take a second.

(Bambi eyes)

AWESOME!

When the plane suddenly speeds up on the runway

....

Because here we go . . .

   AWESOME!

The sound of barely frozen puddles cracking when you step on them

Crisp breezes chip at your cheeks as you **shiver and slide** to school. Blades of grass are stiff with **frosted dew** on their tips, your breath puffs in cold clouds in front of you, and little puddles on the footpath get **that thin film of ice** across the tops, just waiting for you to do what you gotta do.

When you're slip-shuffling half asleep, buried under your backpack, there's just something sweet about stomping those frozen puddles and filling the still and silent walk with a nice crisp **CRACK**.

After you do the deed, you trudge on against the biting wind with an extra spring in your step and **twinkle in your eye**, because you came across the frozen puddle first and you **busted it good**.

Let's face it: That crack is so permanent, **so satisfying**, and so completely

AWESOME!

When someone compliments your new haircut

Haircuts are stressful.

Come on, there are at least **Three Major Worries** when you get your lid trimmed:

1. **Disappearing Choppers**. Have you ever gone to your regular place and found your go-to guy suddenly missing? Talk about a bombshell. On top of the loss, the gang left over is usually tight-lipped on details too. No forwarding address, no new business cards, nothing. They just vanished and left only a few combs floating in the Barbicide for clues. Now it's time to step into the chair with The New Guy and grit your teeth, grab the handlebars, and brace yourself for a rickety journey down a dark mine shaft tunnel of horror. As the lights dim and you close your eyes, you can hear the electric razor firing up in the distance . . .

2. **Doing a New Do**. Asking the stylist to try something new is pretty high up there on the Greatest Fears of All Time List. It's *jusssssst* above three-hour root

canal and *jusssssst* below getting a snake thrown on you when you're sleeping.

3. **Getting One-Upped.** This is where you're getting your haircut and one of your stylist's more loyal customers walks in the door. You can tell they're a somebody because they start dominating conversation while you become a third wheel and your stylist goes superspeed and starts cutting corners. Sure, this doesn't happen too often, but if you've ever been one-upped you know exactly what I'm talking about.

Folks, if you're nodding, you know the stress of getting a haircut. As the stylist peels the nylon apron off your neck and brushes **hair shards** off your back you cautiously check the mirror and scope the new you. Sometimes you strut confidently out of the salon like you're in a shampoo commercial and other times you squint at yourself and frown slightly while **cartoony question marks** pop above your head like bubbles.

On days when you have doubts, that little **"Hey, nice haircut"** compliment can do wonders for your self-esteem. Because, come on, we're all self-conscious about those little patches of scraggly knots up there.

Thanks for saying something.

AWESOME!

Using any item within reach to help grab the remote control so you don't have to move

....

Dusty sunbeams streak through the window while you lie on the couch in a blissful half-asleep cocoon. Sometimes during this **hazy daze** a little voice in your brain politely asks that the TV be turned down or shut right off.

In moments like this there's something satisfying about keeping as much of your body completely relaxed and **perfectly still as possible** while awkwardly grabbing the remote with a rolled-up newspaper, cardboard paper towel tube, or another remote that happens to be closer.

After you stab at it and coax it across the carpet, you do the deed and let a little smile curl on your face as you fade deeper and deeper into your comfy afternoon nap.

AWESOME!

The first couple of hours of the road trip

Full boxes of granola bars, **fresh mix tapes**, and the heady thrill of anticipation get your body ready for a nice long ride. Petrol tank's full, washer fluid's topped up, and your tiny thimble bladder doesn't have a drop in it.

We're flying now.

AWESOME!

When the phone rings and it's somebody you were just thinking about

....

Faces float and fly through our brains.

Kicking pebbles, wearing backpacks, laughing about the school day, **your friends** flicker past you with red cheeks and windswept hair on cool and crisp walks home.

Silverware clinking, gravy boats dripping, **your family** sits in thick holiday jumpers under a sparkly chandelier amongst half-filled wineglasses and steaming bowls of broccoli.

Furnace quietly clicking, clock slowly ticking, **your boy-friend** lies beside you on the patchy corduroy couch in the dark unfinished basement, smiling between kisses and laughs, sharing a moment in a memory.

Somebody's thinking about you right now too.

Give them a call.

AWESOME!

Moving indoor furniture outdoors

....

Forget picnic tables, **plastic chairs**, and patio sets.

No, we're talking about the real deal. We're talking about moving furniture from inside your pad to outside it, and **busting the shackles** of climate control in favour of fresh air and good times.

Feel these beats:

1. **Porch Couch.** Sure, your worn-out duct-tape-and-corduroy couch is out in the elements, but now you get a comfy chill-out spot to watch the world go by. Porch couches are perfect for chilling after class at uni, handing out Halloween lollies, or taking your late night neighbourhood watch shift.

2. **Tailgate Party.** Man, have you seen some of these setups? I'm just an amateur, but sometimes we're talking about the entire lounge room transplanted onto the gravel car park outside the stadium. Pops balances the big screen in the pickup truck while Junior lays a rug down by the barbecue. It's time for grilling.

3. **Backyard Birthday.** Wobbly folding chair legs sink into the grass while basement card tables are wiped off and covered in plastic tablecloths for their annual cameo as Punch Bowl Station or Place We're Cutting The Cake Later.

When you move indoor furniture outdoors you're spreading the party all over the place. Chill out, relax, and put your feet up on the cooler, because it's sunny out and it's time to enjoy the moment.

AWESOME!

When your fries order has a few onion rings stashed in the mix

Dive in.

Scoring some sweet and salty rings hidden in your fries is the fast-food equivalent of **finding a treasure chest** at the bottom of the sea. Suddenly you're an explorer stumbling upon a lost shipwreck way, way down in the darkness. While your friends linger above, you plunge deeper and deeper . . . eventually spotting a coral-covered chest wedged between some slippery rocks.

As your heart thump-thumps you kick the rusty lock and peel open the lid to behold a **glittery sight**. Your face turns on like a torch and your eyes pop open behind the scuba mask as you realise you've uncovered a hidden stash of **crunchy, oily gold**.

There be treasure in these fries.

AWESOME!

The Big Night Nap

···

The Big Night Nap or Disco Nap is any nap you take before going out for a big night.

When you nail this warm-up nap perfectly, you end up with a long memorable evening without dog yawns, **wristwatch glances**, and early cave-ins.

Now, that doesn't mean Big Night Naps are easy to pull off. No, no, the truth is you gotta be careful in that late-afternoon **Napping Danger Zone**:

1. **The Power Nap.** Top of the charts. This is the perfectly executed twenty-minute power up that fills your energy bar and gets you ready to take on the world.
2. **The Call-Waiting Nap.** Your plans aren't firmed up so you leave your mobile phone beside you. This forces you to pop up to answer text messages and take groggy phone calls.
3. **The Choreographed Nap.** This is where you convince all your friends to take a Big Night Nap too. You know them well and realise they'll zonk out early if they're not in the game. Do like Parker Lewis and synchronise watches.

4. **The Neverending Nap.** Whoops! You were gonna do a quick snooze but your body had other plans. You groggily kick off your socks as your phone buzzes on your dresser. You're going straight to morning now. Expect a 4 a.m. wake-up call.

5. **The Extend-O-Night Nap.** You head out to someone's house without napping but start losing steam as everyone else is revving up. So you head upstairs and take a quick power snooze on the bed full of jackets. You don't have to be eight years old to pull this move off. You'll be back in the game in no time.

So . . . save 'em for New Year's, **save 'em for slumber parties,** save 'em for nights you need extra juice. Yes, when you go down early to **get down late** it's a beautiful moment of party planning that we like to call

AWESOME!

Hilarious last-minute Halloween costumes

....

Back at uni, I remember walking up to my friend Mike's house on Halloween and seeing him frantically painting **bright red briefs** onto a pair of nice blue jeans. He was really going at it, too—slapping the wet brush all over the crotch and pockets, wagging his tongue out like a dog on the front lawn.

Of course, an hour later he showed up to the party as Superman. And though he didn't leap any tall buildings in a single bound, he did manage to drink most of the punch bowl faster than a speeding bullet.

More important, his last-minute Halloween costume got us all laughing. The best ones do that:

- **Professional Baseball Player**. This is where you dig through your closet and peel out that old sweat-smelling jersey and orange foam hat from Little League. Throw on your baseball glove and paint some thick black lines under your eyes and you're good to go.
- **Sandwich**. My friend Brian once slapped a piece of bread on his chest and another on his back

and went as a sandwich. You've heard of a Quarter Pounder, right? Well this was a two-hundred-pounder.

- **Vending Machine**. Here's where you duct-tape little bags of chips and chocolate bars all over your body. If your party's working properly, they'll be ripped off you within ten minutes of getting there.

- **The Random Closet Mishmash with a Funny Name.** You've got a purple tie, dark shades, and leather pants so you go as a Club-Going Comedian With A Black Eye. You've got a bridesmaid dress, oven mitts, and a tiara, so you go as Lounge Singer Baking Biscuits For A Bachelorette Party. You get the idea.

- **Jabba the Hutt.** Time to laze around on the couch in a green sleeping bag.

- **The Walk of Shame**. Simply wear a man's shirt over your dress clothes, mess up your hair, and carry a pair of high heels in your hand. For guys, try a backwards, inside-out shirt, sideways bedhead, and your shoes on the wrong feet.

- **A Terrible Record Collection**. My friend Alec once bought a milk crate of old records for a quarter from a garage sale. They were in horrible condition, but the price was right so he took them home. For Halloween he safety-pinned most of them on himself and went as A Terrible Record Collection.

It was a good laugh, but since he couldn't really move, he ending up spending most of the party whisper-singing "Monster Mash" to himself on a futon.

- **Grapes.** Boy, if you've got some purple or green balloons lying around, have we got a costume for you.

- **Yourself.** This is where you arrive at the party completely unprepared, but rather than fess up you just tell people you're going as yourself this year. Then whenever someone says, "But that's not a costume," you say, "Maybe it is, my friend . . . maybe it is," and then give a really exaggerated wink.

Okay listen, when somebody puts an amazing amount of time and effort into a **kick-arse costume**, that's worth celebrating. Nobody here denies that. All we're saying is if you manage to scramble around your house at the last minute and get us all laughing with your hilariously creative costume, then that's complete admirable.

It's simply commendable.

It's downright respectable.

And we all know it's just totally

AWESOME!

When company events are scheduled on company time

Thanks, boss.

When you observe the **safe haven** of our evenings and weekends by scheduling company events during company hours, we're loving you lots. Because come on, we all have lots going on after work—clothes need washing, family needs visiting, and the kids have a sports tournament out of town.

So throw that **company picnic** on a sunny Friday afternoon. We'll get the Frisbee going with the assistant manager and gather around the wobbly buffet table to try the secretary's homemade potato-and-egg salad or the vice president's expensive bakery-bought brownies. Get those **team-building exercises** motoring on Monday morning, when we all need coffee jolts and trust falls to perk us up for the week. And toss your **recognition lunches** in the middle of the week, when a chilled-out Wednesday barbecue helps get us through to the other side.

When company events are scheduled on company time, we get a magical little moment where the photocopier stops, **lines slow down**, and we all relax for a couple of chilled-out hours of

AWESOME!

Good escalator etiquette

You stand on that side. We'll walk on this side.

AWESOME!

When you think you're out of clean underwear but then you find one more pair

Admit it.

You've done the sniff test.

Sure, while shuffling through a **mish-mashed drawer** of balled-up socks and **stained undershirts** a few minutes ago you started panicking when you thought there was nothing left. Soon your mind started racing into Plan B's and C's:

1. **Rock the commando.** Should you just skip underwear altogether? After all, it seems to be what the fates are telling you. On the plus side, you can leave the house right away and avoid being late for work. On the downside, zips.

2. **Pull a dirty pair out of the basket.** Maybe you're scoffing now, but we know you've been there, too. Hey, sometimes you can totally justify it to yourself: "It's probably air-dried itself clean by now", "I didn't sweat the day I wore these", or the classic, "I know, I'll just wear them inside out. I am a genius."

3. **Borrower beware.** Whoa, whoa, whoa, over the line. Move on.
4. **Go buy some.** Unless you're living in the remote rocky outskirts of a distant mining town, camping up north at a lakeside cabin, or getting changed after hours, there are decent odds a local discount chain has a plastic-wrapped three-pack with your name on it.

Yeah, it's a stressful scene when the clock's clicking, **the baby's crying**, and you're running late for work while running around pantsless. But that's why it's sweet when you keep digging and digging and digging and digging and eventually unearth a terribly twisted, **torn and tattered**, mothball-smelling pair of ratty old underwear you haven't worn in years.

AWESOME!

Your Almost Name

....

It's what your parents were going to call you **but didn't**.

Flipping through baby books, **chatting at bedtime**, you better believe your folks had alternate identities in mind before you borned out. They thought about nicknames, **short forms**, and tributes. They thought about spelling, rhyming, and meanings. Basically, they thought and hoped and wished all kinds of things for you even before you made it here.

Sometimes when you find out your Almost Name it feels odd and uncomfortable—like putting on an itchy shirt, **clenching your fist after waking up**, or walking out of a movie and realising your foot's asleep. Maybe you let your mind wander and daydream about a new life where your Almost Name takes top billing and your nicknames, identity, and major life choices are all dramatically affected. You wonder how your life could be different—would you be more confident? **Less passionate?** More artsy? Less annoying?

Nothing's the same when you're Nancy.

Everything changes when you're Chuck.

Now, my Almost Name is Paul. Yes, it was a close call and my parents switched over to Neil at the last minute. I'm pretty sure **Neil Diamond** or **Neil Armstrong** got the name bouncing around their brains like a ping-pong ball. But somehow Paul got tossed in the can before I showed up and my entire Paul Life got tossed with it.

And maybe that's one reason Almost Names are so great: **They remind us how lucky we are we didn't get them.** I mean, it's just fun letting Almost Names add frames and borders to our lives . . . because it helps us feel a little more sure of ourselves and a lot more

AWESOME!

Getting the keys to your first apartment

....

Welcome to the throne.

For years you toiled as a lowly pauper under the rule of another castle. Sure, maybe the leaders of your old kingdom ruled with a fair hand but there were times your ideas and their ideas clashed. They wanted quiet, you wanted a **pet jester**, they wanted curfews, you wanted courtyard parties, they wanted bunk beds in the barracks, you wanted your own tower.

Now you've moved out and got yourself your own place. Sure, the moat's in rough shape and the stables are a write-off, but at least it reflects your personality and your taste. You've got a new responsibility and can do anything you want: put **purple tapestries** on the stone walls, hold court with new boyfriends, or skip the castle kitchen to go out for turkey drumsticks and a few glasses of mead.

Long live the king. Long live the queen.

Long live your new kingdom of

AWESOME!

The sound of aeroplane toilet flushes

······································

I was on a long flight not too long ago, one where they turn the lights out for most of the trip and everybody is just lying like jelly all over their seats fast asleep. Legs propped up over armrests, **seats reclined into laps,** and headphones, blankets, and eye masks creating cocoon-like defences against all light, sound, and touch.

Frankly, I don't like flights like this because I feel really uncomfortable. I think I'm going to wake people up and bother them. I feel like **I'm hanging out in a nursery** and I've finally got all the babies asleep, and now I just have to sit in a rocking chair in the corner taking quiet, calculated breaths until the sun rises.

It's very stressful.

I have always been paranoid about waking people up. When I was younger and would come home late, I would take about twenty minutes to get from the driveway into my bed. I tiptoed up the walk, slid my house key in the door very slowly, took my **shoes off outside,** and crept upstairs to the bathroom like a burglar. Often I wouldn't even flush until morning, preferring to **let my business simmer overnight** rather than wake somebody up with the sound of it zooming through walls on its way out of the house.

On the aeroplane I don't tilt my seat back too far because I think I might crowd the person behind me. I walk down the aisle very carefully, grabbing chairs and overhead compartments for support so that a sudden jolt of turbulence doesn't knock me into a sleeping grandma's lap. I have brief visions of shattering her hip and **sending her dentures flying** into someone's glass of wine.

It is because of my attempts to keep really quiet on these **Voyages of the Subconscious** that I am fascinated by the toilets in the aeroplane.

First of all, they exist! The fact that you can go to the bathroom on an aeroplane is pretty novel. I bet nobody expected that a hundred years ago. Can you imagine two sailors looking over the front rails of their massive ocean liner in the early 1900s, one of them pointing way up in the clouds and whispering to the other, "One day a man will take a crap up there." No, me neither.

Anyway, after we get over the fact that these bathrooms exist, let's talk about **that amazing flush.** You do your thing, close that lid, hit that little plastic button, and a second later there's a full five seconds of giant, full-force, vacuum-sucking noises. It's so loud it's unbelievable—like a transport truck full of silverware crashing into a pyramid of wineglasses on the dirt patch between two World War I trenches.

See, apparently aeroplanes use something called **vacuum toilets**. I guess these big guys are perfect for the job because they don't use much water and are fairly low maintenance. Just one little side effect, though: When you flush them it sounds like the world is exploding.

Personally, I love that beautifully loud aeroplane toilet flush. And since I can't very well leave a gift bowl for the next passenger, I'm forced to press the button. The noise of that flush undoubtedly **wakes up the last few rows** on the aeroplane every time, so I have no choice but to confront my fears.

So I say thanks, aeroplane toilet flush. Your whooshing, vacuum-packed boomflush wakes the whole world up.

AWESOME!

Actually pointing out a constellation in outer space

....

Growing up between streetlights and **neon pizza signs** it was pretty rare to stare up at a dark sky full of sparkly stars.

Now, if we went camping or up to a friend's cottage, that was a different story. That's when we could zip open our tent or lie on the dock and gaze up at the **twinkly beauty** above us all. We'd just tilt our necks, drop our jaws, and wonder how big it was, how far it went, and what the **tentacled, saliva-covered aliens** looking back at us were thinking.

It didn't happen too often, but every once in a while somebody would pick out a few bright stars and point out a constellation way up there, light-years away, **worlds apart**, and sparkling for all eternity. We'd hear stories about bulls, belt buckles, and the private affairs of many Greek gods.

Of course, I could only ever see one thing up there myself: **The Big Dipper** aka **The Plough**. Sometimes I thought I'd see something else only to have an older kid tell me I was looking at a plane, a blinking satellite, or occasionally the moon.

That's why when you actually point out a constellation in outer space you feel like a genius with a PhD in **Good Eyesight**. You're no longer the dude responsible for finding marshmallow roasting sticks, grabbing insect repellent from the tent, or dumping a pail of water onto the fire before we head to bed. No, now you're a worldly space explorer raising your eyebrows and pointing out the window as we all fly forward through the darkness.

AWESOME!

Whipping down the hill really fast on your bike after pedaling hard all the way up

Wind whips through your hair and **smacks your cheeks** as you scream down the slope at the rip-rocketing speed of

AWESOME!

Watching a movie in the basement with a group of friends

It's better in the basement.

Give us the stained couches demoted from the family room. Give us those plastic walls full of pink insulation. Give us those cold floors and thin carpets.

Give us that dark cave hidden from the outside world.

Give us a group of friends hanging out.

And give us a screwball comedy.

Yes, it's time to order that pizza, fall into the squishy couch, **pile pillows against one another**, and pass the fuzzball blankets. It's time to enjoy a good movie with a group of friends—ideally featuring several of these characters:

- **The Waiter.** Sure, the host usually covers this job— filling popcorn, pouring Pepsis—but if the gang's supertight someone else can take it on. If you know your friend's pantry well and they don't mind you raccooning around, feel free to take orders and go digging for gold.
- **The Punch Line.** This is the person who adds the live commentary from the corner of the couch. He

generally tries to top the characters on-screen and his favourite line is *"That's* gotta hurt!"

- **The Revealer.** The Revealer saw this movie already. You find that out the first time they say "Shhhhhh! Good scene coming up, good scene."

- **The Maestro.** This is a high-pressure role that involves owning the remote control for the entire movie. The Maestro is responsible for determining which bathroom breaks are pause-worthy and when to rewind and rewatch an important scene. Also, they must be comfortable cranking the volume if The Revealer ("Good scene!") and The Punch Line ("Gotta hurt!") start talking too loudly.

- **The Graphics Judge.** Does that plane crash look fake? Do those dinosaurs look real? The Graphics Judge offers instant analysis on all special effects scenes.

- **The Snoozer.** No matter how loud the explosions, how tight the plot, or how dramatic the chase scene, The Snoozer can be counted on to let out a few quiet snores just as things are getting good. Sometimes it's best to seat The Snoozer on the same faraway couch as The Person Who Covers Their Eyes And Gasps During Scary Scenes and The Person Who Cries All The Time, Even If It's Not A Sad Film.

- **The Dimmer.** This person is obsessed with movie theatre atmosphere. Ten seconds into the movie they frantically start a mad dash to turn off every light in the room. This seems like a good idea until someone has to blindman's bluff their way up the rickety stairs to go to the bathroom.

Now, every group's got their own cast of characters. It's good to **love them all** and it's good to love those moments.

After all, friends grow up and graduate, **some people change and roll on,** and life wheels and deals us in all directions. So love those late nights in sixth grade with soft drink and double cheese pizzas. Love those 4 a.m. Fridays in high school when everyone's friends and **everything's funny.**

Just remember those long nights, **strong nights,** and staying-up-till-dawn nights. Smile hard at the smiles, laugh loud at the laughs, and always enjoy those basement movie memories . . . with your basement movie friends.

AWESOME!

Your tongue

Babies are funny.

While I was zooming down the highway with my friend Agostino recently he broke into a story about his one-year-old daughter. Apparently while feeding her a bowl of **mushy peas** she suddenly started sticking her tongue out, **slowly and suspiciously** peering down at it, and then wiggling it around.

It was like she suddenly came to the starstruck realisation that **"I can control this thing!"**

And what an amazing day that must be, **for you,** for me, for anybody. After all, we grow up inside these flabby blobs of flexy muscles, whirring organs, and gurgling body parts, and then discover what everything does along the way.

The mysteries of your tongue are sort of discovered along the way too. And what beautiful mysteries they are:

1. **Tongue got your cat.** Yes, the muscles at the back of your tongue help make certain sounds while talking like hard *g*'s and *c*'s. Try saying the word *go* or *cat* really slowly and you'll feel that pink puppy push across the roof of your mouth.

2. **Bubble blower.** Hey, that wad of chewing gum ain't gonna balloon into a thin n' shaky pink bubble on its own.

3. **Whistle while you work.** Think of your mouth like the cold garage where your lips and tongue come together to jam after school. Your lips make a small opening and your tongue gets the bumping grooves going. Also works for singing.

4. **Taste the rainbow.** When you're a one-year-old baby you've got around ten thousand taste buds covering your tongue and when you're a wrinkly old fart you've got around five thousand. These tiny flavour detectors are why mushy bananas and macaroni taste so good when you're a kid and bloody steaks and olives do the job when you're older. On top of all that, your tongue helps move food to your teeth and then down the gully for digestion. It's basically the whistle-blowing traffic cop of your body.

5. **Clean your fur.** If your entire body is covered in fur your tongue helps you clean off instead of taking a bath.

6. **French kissing.** Apparently swapping spit is a common gesture of affection throughout the animal kingdom, as lovers kiss with their tongues in jungles, deserts, and bat caves throughout the world. Evolutionary biologist Thierry Lode even argues

that tongue kissing has a real function—to explore a partner's immune system through their saliva. Yeah, I know: hot.

Once upon a time **you discovered your tongue** with a profound sense of eye-widening wonder and amazement. Over time you began using its magical powers to try new foods, learn how to speak, sing in the car, or snuggle up with a young love.

So today give three cheers to that fleshy pink slab of greatness sitting inside your **hot, disgusting mouth**. Use its noble powers to sit back and scream forward one big booming word with me . . .

AWESOME!

The air just before a thunderstorm

Warm wind whips and whistles down the streets sending cigarette butts, **crumpled receipts**, and dry leaves swirling in all directions. Specks of dust glow **in deep sunbeam** tints as dark clouds shuffle in the sky. There's a warm and wet sense of electric anticipation as lightning bolts **flash silently** in the distance, dogs bark in the background, and everyone races for cover.

You hear the nylon swish of umbrellas popping open, the scrape of **plastic chairs** dragging across patios, and the adrenaline buzzing before the first big boom.

Here come the jumbo drops.

AWESOME!

Accidentally doing something really good in sports

I'm terrible at sports.

When I was a kid I retired from soccer after just one season. In my final game I took a booted ball right to the face which **snapped my glasses** in two and caused me to crash to the field in a wet, goobery mess. Unfortunately, since we were low on players and couldn't forfeit the big playoff game, I was forced to hang out on the field, blind and drippy, until the whistle blew.

And it wasn't just soccer either. I hung up the cleats after a season of baseball too. Somehow I managed to bat fourteenth in the lineup and lead my team in **hit by pitches**. This was less because I crowded the plate with gritted teeth and steely determination and more because most **twelve-year-olds** can't pitch straight and I have **extremely slow reflexes**.

Since I'm so bad at sports, I tend to overcelebrate any type of tiny sports victory I can get. I'm not talking about shooting a buzzer-beating three-pointer or catching a winning touchdown. No, I'm talking about any **teeny-weeny play** during the game where I get to feel like I actually did something right for a second.

Here are some of my faves:

1. **The Air Hockey Self-Score**. This is where your opponent fires the plastic puck so hard it bounces off your end and scores on their own net. Fist pumps all around.

2. **The Accidental Pool Shot**. Here's where you aim for the six ball in the corner pocket but miss completely and send the cue ball spinning wildly around the table until it accidentally bumps another ball into a completely different pocket. We'll take it.

3. **Rim Rollers**. Okay, over to basketball. This is when your shot bounces off the side of the backboard and clangs around for ten seconds, bouncing in every direction, before eventually, reluctantly, spinning around the rim and slowly falling into the basket.

4. **The Lucky Golf Bounce**. The only way my terrible golf shot is landing on the fairway is if it smacks off a tree trunk in the forest and pops back out. Bouncing a hundred feet in the air off the paved golf cart path might also do the trick.

5. **The Slow Strike**. Do you ever go bowling? If you're as bad as I am you love that moment when your ball barely nudges a corner pin and causes a slow-motion domino effect that eventually gives you a strike. Time for a Stage Dance or Hulk Hogan pose.

6. **The Tennis Drop-off**. Here's my favourite one of all.
   Yes, when you win a point in tennis by hitting the
   ball into the net and having it immediately fall
   over and die on the other side, that's just perfect.

Now, I know what you're thinking: These are all **terrible
cheap shots** no athlete would be proud to score. But I'm no
athlete, people. I'll take my cheap shots when I get 'em if I
get 'em. And, you know, maybe these little flukes are just the
result of intense wanting and willing for success and therefore not flukes at all. No, maybe they're deliberate interven-
tions on the part of the Sports Gods in order to motivate us
to keep on pushing.

AWESOME!

Tuning the radio station perfectly so there's absolutely no static

....

I'm a terrible tuner.

Yeah, I'm the guy twiddling clock radio dials before bed every night with scrunched-up eyebrows. When I do end up on a **crystal-clear station** it usually isn't the one I was aiming for or I end up accidentally using my body as an antenna so the sound gets fuzzy the second I move my hand away.

For a second it's clear and then it's schzzzteeeeeeeeyiiiiiiiio-OoOoOssZZZZT.

You'd definitely find these moments over in *The Book of Annoying*, that nonexistent netherlist that also features: Someone shaking your hand with freshly wet hands from the bathroom, **Bendy straws that crack at the bendy part**, and Getting the wobbly table at a restaurant.

Brother, that's why nothing's as nice as landing perfectly on your radio station of choice after twiddling that little dial for a few quick moments. When you nail it just right, slowly move your hand away, **pause for station identification**, and quickly click the switch over to **Alarm,** you're loving it lots.

See, radio waves float and fly through our lives sending highway traffic reports, **wacky morning DJs**, and bumping bass beats bouncing around the air like magic. It's up to us to catch them like butterflies with our thin antennas, **dusty clock radios,** and determined little fingers driven to get the job done.

AWESOME!

Waking up really thirsty in the morning and finding a glass of water within reach

Maybe you scoffed a salty bag of chips before bed, drank a bit too much at the bars, or woke up on a friend's **old pull-out couch** with a mouthful of dust and cat hair.

Either way, when you blink your crusty eyes open and feel your mouth scratching like **sandpaper**, there's nothing finer than spotting a calmly waiting glass of water sitting just in front of your face.

After silently congratulating the **You of Last Night** for good planning, you smile slowly, chug it fast, and snuggle back into your dreamy slumbers.

AWESOME!

The sound of steaks hitting a hot grill

Tssssssssssssssssss.

    AWESOME!

Eating the crusts of the sandwich first to save the middle part for last

Nobody wants to finish on a downer.

If you aren't careful, the last bite of your lunch will be a big chomp of **dry crusts and lettuce scraps**. Your mouth will finish on a lame and boring note with the delicious middle bites from minutes ago lost in a dry, crusty daze.

Don't let it happen to you!

Put your time in at the beginning, sacrifice early nibbles and take care of the corners, and set yourself up for a deliciously fresh and soft **ham-and-cheesy finale** to finish off your lunch.

AWESOME!

Sneezing three or more times in a row

Sometimes sneezes hit you and hit you hard.

Unless you're rolling around in a pile of cut grass or sleeping on a pillow filled with **pepper and cat hair**, it usually starts completely out of nowhere. You feel that tickle deep in your nose. Just a tiny little quiver way, way up there, near where your eyeball connects to your brain. You squint a bit, pull your hand to your mouth, and then BOOOOM! Your eyes squeeze tightly, your face crunches together, and it screams down your face at the speed of sneeze, exploding out of your mouth in an ugly climax of wetness in all directions.

Despite the look of it, sneezing can feel pretty great. Not only does repeated sneezing give you a weird, spacey head rush, but it can also be quite refreshing. Sinuses get cleaned out, nose hairs get a windy blowdown, and you end up firing whatever was irritating you out of your nasal cavity like a cannon, sending it flying across the room in a flailing **I Must Get This Out Of Me** overreaction.

Now, although sneezes are usually a surprise, there are times when you know they're in there and you **just want them to leave**. What's worse than that frustratingly stubborn sneeze? I'm talking about the kind that pauses all conversation, leaving your friends stuck grimacing and watching you writhe in an agitated **Potentially Sneezing Soon State**, trying to force the sneeze locked in your nose in or out.

It's awkward.

That's why it feels great to let that booming sneeze out, preferably in a punctuated rat a tat tat sequence of three or more sneezes for the full effect. Tiny mousesqueak sneezes, **booming dogbark sneezes,** whatever your style, that's cool, that's cool. Pretty soon your body is buzzing, your sinuses are sparkling, and your head pipes are all vacuumed clean.

AWESOME!

The smell of Play-Doh

Sniff up some fumes and get ready for a **brain cell party**.

Yes, those sleeping memories from long ago will wake up and **bounce and crash** around your head as you close your eyes and let that **salty sweetness** take you back to kindergarten.

Fade to black and remember slightly greasy hands with bits in the fingernails, remember mixing all the colours together until they turned **purply-brown**, remember rolling out lots of cold lopsided worms, and remember the taste-test incident that resulted in a cold and salty mouth.

Yes, that smell of Play-Doh takes us way back to the old school. If you're sniffing up what we're putting down, then you're an old fool **who's so cool**. If you wanna get back, let us show you the way.

Whoomp, there it is.

Lemme hear you say

AWESOME!

Junk drawers

....

"Honey, have you seen my measuring tape?"

"I think it's in that drawer in the kitchen with the scissors, matches, bobby pins, Scotch tape, nail clippers, barbecue tongs, garlic press, extra buttons, old birthday cards, **soy sauce packets**, thick rubber bands, stack of Christmas serviettes, stained take-out menus, old mobile-phone chargers, instruction booklet for the VCR, some assorted loose change, an incomplete deck of cards, extra chain links for a watch, a half-finished pack of cough drops, **a Scrabble piece I found while vacuuming**, dead batteries we aren't fully sure are dead yet, a couple of screws in a tiny plastic bag left over from the bookshelf, that lock with the forgotten combination, a square of carefully folded aluminium foil, an expired pack of gum, a key to our old house, a toaster warranty card, phone numbers for unknown people, **used birthday candles**, novelty bottle openers, a barbecue lighter, and that one tiny little spoon."

"Thanks, honey."

AWESOME!

Hot cream and a straight razor on your neck at the barbershop

Okay, first off, it **just feels great**. Because really, how often do you get something nice and warm smeared on the back of your neck? Speak up if you're getting this action somewhere else, because **we're all ears**. For me, it's only when I go to that old-school barbershop—the one with the red-and-white striped pole out in front, the old dog-eared *Sports Illustrated*s from the 1990s sitting on the table, and no formal system at all for figuring out who's next in line.

Secondly, how cool is that straight razor blade? Maybe it's a bit dangerous. Maybe it's unhygienic. But it sure is a giant blade, is what I'm saying. You have to respect a man who can wield such a mighty and **powerful weapon**. I mean, scissors I could handle. Sure, if you let me cut your daughter's hair, I'd probably give her a **messy faux-hawk** by accident, but the point is that scissors don't scare me. Now, that giant blade is another story. It would take a lot to convince me to slice that thing across a man's neck for the first time.

Finally, how close is that shave? Dude, it's like you've never had hair on your neck before. Suddenly you're transformed into a **ten-year-old boy**. And you know, you sort of felt like one anyway, because the barber is generally older than your dad and dispenses life advice pretty liberally. Either that or he talks about boxing like in the movies.

Now, the only real problem with the hot shaving cream and a straight razor on your neck is that it's pretty tough to find these days. Which is sad, since apparently straight-razor shaving has been around approximately **six thousand more years** than any of us. So I say let's bring it back, folks. Let's keep demanding that our neck beards be trimmed with the slice of a nice blade. And then maybe people at barbershop school will line up to learn **The Art of the Knife**.

AWESOME!

Stumbling on an elusive re-run of your favourite TV show

This champion channel flip can happen in three big ways:

1. **The Missing Link.** This is when you suddenly realise you haven't seen this episode before—ever! You love the show, you're a huge fan, you've seen most episodes ten times . . . but now you landed on the missing link. Maybe you always knew this episode existed but didn't get to witness it until today. You know you landed on a missing link if you find yourself saying things like "Is this the backwards episode?," "So *that's* when she got braces," or "Ahhhh, now I get that joke mentioned later in the series. My soul is at peace."

2. **The Full Fave.** Here's when you find your favourite episode of the series and get giddy with anticipation. Maybe it's The Soup Nazi on *Seinfeld*, the time Carlton gets cut from the frat, or that dark day when Jessie Spano takes too many caffeine pills. Chances are good you've seen the end of this one twenty times and that's exactly what makes the full version such a sweet release.

3. **The Surprise Marathon.** This gem involves crashing on a surprise re-run of your favourite show on a Sunday afternoon. You watch till the end and then are surprised when just before you flick off the TV . . . another one starts up again! You raise your eyebrows and smile before settling back into your couch dent and checking the local listings out of curiosity. That's when your blood starts bubbling with excitement as you realise you just stumbled on a surprise marathon.

People, when this happens it's a **great big rush** of excitement in the middle of your family room. You've gotta dim those lights, pop that corn, and stare deeply at the glittery gold moment before you.

AWESOME!

When you open a book to the exact page you were looking for

You cracked the case.

When you pop open that textbook, **flip open the yellow pages**, or split the spine of that novel right to the spot you're looking for, it's a beautiful moment.

Suddenly you transform into a gloomy **trench-coat-wearing detective** who solves the case just by glancing at the crime scene. Yes, the street's been taped off, someone's crying under a blanket on the curb, and the city police are filling out **witness statements** on their notepads.

That's when you peel up in a navy blue squad car, calmly light up a cigarette, and then stare at the surrounding buildings for a few minutes with cold, emotionless eyes.

Then you calmly walk back to your cruiser, **smile softly**, and roll your window down at the local police.

"Page 127," you mutter with a half smile, before screaming away down the wet city roads.

AWESOME!

Catching food in your mouth

Toss it mean and catch it clean.

Drop that jaw, tilt that head, and let's get down to business:

- **Level 1: Pop Practice.** It's important to start small with popcorn. There are no penalties for misses here, since the corn is light and doesn't collect much dust if it hits the ground. This is a baby step and will take time to master, but it's an important rite of passage before hitting the next levels. This level also covers marshmallows and Cheerios. (+5 points)

- **Level 2: The Grape Beyond.** Yup, next step is big ol' grapes. Usually someone on the other end of the couch is munching a vine in their own little bowl. If you're feeling a bit hungry, simply drop your mouth and tap the couch cushion while saying "Uhn! Uhn! Uhnnnnn!" to get their attention. Soon a cold, hard grape should be flying at you fast. If the toss is good, make sure you catch it perfectly. Raspberries and strawberries are in Level 2 as well. (+10 points)

- **Level 3: Dog On A Bone.** This extremely advanced move involves catching something larger than your entire mouth. An apple, peeled orange, or corn on a cob are good targets. You need to time the molar chomp perfectly and be prepared for embarrassing T-shirt stains and occasional black eyes. (+25 points)

Yes, when you catch food in your mouth, you're suddenly sitting high on top of the snack-eating universe. You've just combined equal parts laziness and **athletic ability** in a daring couch potato feat the likes of which this basement has never seen before. So when you nail it smoothly you know what to do.

Chomp it loud and chew it proud.

AWESOME!

Making it halfway

Maybe you're running on the **treadmill** when you catch the clock tick past the middle of your **sweaty jog**. Maybe you're painting the nursery when you realise you're right in the middle of your pregnancy. Or maybe you're on a long **Sunday drive** to visit a hometown friend when you pass that rusty petrol station halfway down the highway.

Yes, it sure is sweet making it halfway anywhere. It means you got started, **you gave it a shot**, and now you're doing it, baby.

When you make it halfway, take a moment to **smile and enjoy** where you're at. Because sure, there's a lot in that rearview mirror, but there's so much around the bend too.

Let's keep going.

AWESOME!

Realising you still remember your childhood friend's phone number

Etched and sketched into the spiderweb recesses of our brains are all kinds of cold-storage items and **garage sale knickknacks** we don't really use anymore. But once in a while it's fun to reach back, back, way back, and discover that our creaky treasure chests are holding bits of buried gold.

Realising you still remember old phone numbers gives a great smile-and-sunshine vibe. Lips curl, eyes twinkle, and memory reels start whirring on the rusty projector as you remember **dialing those digits**, day after day, day after day, day after day. Making plans for the park, **grumbling about teachers**, whispering about cute classmates late at night, you just suddenly remember those times, those moments, and those old, old friends.

Dial them up today.

AWESOME!

Laughing so hard
you start crying

....

It's a beautiful moment.

Your friend suddenly starts shaking her head while laughing so hard little streams of **salty tears** start running down her cheeks. She covers her mouth with her hands as her face turns red—and you can see **shiny reflections sparkle** in her glittery wet eyes. Big booms bounce off walls until she eventually slows down, gasps for air while **wet sniffling**, smiling widely, and regaining her composure.

And then she looks you right in the eyes and smiles. And you look her right in the eyes and smile. And your sides hurt and **you shake your head** and you feel like you might pee your pants . . .

And it starts all over again . . .

AWESOME!

Wearing your favourite pair of underwear and nobody knows

You know the ones.

Maybe they fit perfectly, **don't ride up**, and leave nothing bulging over the edges. Yes, they flatter in all the right places and all the right spaces, baby.

Or maybe you're a **straightlaced Sally** and they're your wildly inappropriate pair that turn you into a G-String Rebel. Caution: **RED HOT!**

Or . . . maybe they're just the perfect shade of the **perfect colour** and you've had them in your dresser drawer for ages. Maybe they remind you of a special moment or a memory that's fun to keep to yourself all day. Maybe they just give you a little more confidence for that speech or first date.

But whatever yours are and whatever they look like, there's something great about giving yourself a smile. Because hey, wearing your favourite underwear when nobody knows is a cheap way to **think positive thoughts** without doing anything too earth-shattering.

It's just a simple thing for a simple smile.

AWESOME!

When you're not the new guy anymore

··

The first day was scary.

When you opened the door everything was a **giant swirling abyss** of new teachers, new faces, new rules, and new places. So you tiptoed in smiling and shaking hands, learning passwords and policies, and staring around the busy playground trying to find someone to eat lunch with.

It wasn't your fault but you were last to join the team, **you were last getting in the game,** you were last one signing in, and no one knew your name.

So you just put your head down and gave it a shot. **You tried and tried and tried.** You felt like you didn't belong here so you worked a bit harder than the next guy. Maybe you organised a neighbourhood garage sale, **maybe you helped the bullpen in the clutch,** maybe you bailed us all out of a big meeting, or maybe you threw a backyard party...with a special touch.

(Special touches may or may not include: big bowls of fizzy punch teetering on wobbly picnic tables, **veggie hotdogs** cooking to a crispy finish on their own grill, or baking anything rich and chocolatey for dessert.)

Soon you noticed you were starting to fit in and there were beers after the ballgame, **lab partners in chemistry class**, and new friends in the playground. Somebody asked you for help one day, a nickname slowly evolved, and a **dirty inside joke** got everyone laughing for weeks.

One day someone even newer than you started up and while they squeezed nervously beside you at the lunch table it slowly hit you.

You aren't the new guy anymore.

You fit in just fine.

AWESOME!

The sniff test

Works on underwear, milk, and babies.
    If it smells bad, it's bad.
    If it smells good, it's
    AWESOME!

When your windscreen wipers match the beat of the song you're listening to

Cruising home from a friend's place, **driving the kids to school**, rolling home on the highway, you smile softly and focus on the road as your head bops to the stereo.

Suddenly clouds cover the sky, **the air gets heavy**, and big drops start pitter-pattering your windscreen. Snare drum staccatos fill your car's cabin and you quickly flip on your windscreen wipers.

But if you're lucky this is when the **groove starts grooving** and your **car starts moving** as you notice your wipers are timed perfectly to the stereo beats. Yes, without even trying, your rusty bucket's become a pitch-perfect concert hall on the highway. Chattery crowds start filing down the aisles, the balcony fills up, and the lights slowly dim as whispers fill the air.

Hands clapping, fingers tapping, you click your turn signal on so a little high hat and **dashboard disco light** join your dance party on wheels. With your body bumping and your brain thumping, your **one-man jam band** rocks out in the fast lane.

It feels like everything's coming together for a great **big booming moment**. You sing along as cosmic energy swirls and the universe gives a little wink to let you know everything's unfolding according to plan.

AWESOME!

Sitting on your freshly made bed and admiring your work after cleaning your room

Once again your room is at the top of its game.

No more tripping on crumpled **jeans flowers** on your way to the light switch. No more grabbing random jumpers off your desk only to notice **streaky mustard stains** later in the day. Nope, no more dust bunnies, no more dried-out pudding cups, and no more bedside tables jammed with junk.

As you sit on your bed and look around you enjoy a brief moment of living in a **furniture magazine**. Crisp and clean, free and fresh, you can practically hear the phone ringing and a fast-talking group of Scandinavian engineers begging to come over and study your work.

Let them come over and stare down their glasses at your **tightly crisped bedsheets**. Let them make clipboard notes on your clean-carpet vacuum streaks. And let them swipe their lab coat sleeves on your dust-free couch seats.

Yes, you killed a few hours cleaning up the joint and now your place is looking sparkling and special. Stop for a moment to let it all soak in.

AWESOME!

Eating biscuits like Cookie Monster

....

It sure is a sign of **gluttonous satisfaction** when you find your-self home alone, slouching on the couch in front of the TV with your eyes half open, a steady trail of biscuit crumbs making its way from your mouth onto your shirt and pants, **chocolate smears** on your lips and fingers, and the telltale bis-cuit package lying beside you, the plastic tray peeled all the way out of the bag, entire rows lying vacant except for a bit of brown dust and maybe a **rogue chocolate chip** or two.

Yes, it's satisfying alright, because many delicious biscuits were eaten, without witnesses, in a very quick and steady stream by shoving them into your mouth, chewing a few times, and then swallowing quickly to make room for the next one. You're a monster and you love it.

Eating biscuits like Cookie Monster is great because, more than anything, it represents freedom. Yes, free thought takes you to the pantry, free will makes you grab that biscuit package, and free re-runs keep you company while you sit down and enjoy. You're the **Executive Chef** in your personal Dessert Kitchen here. Just tell me that's not liberating.

I mean, sure, we all know it's not the greatest idea to eat a pile of biscuits just before bed, but that's not the point. The point is: You can do it. Yes, you've come a long way from the portion-controlled snacks you got when you were a kid, maybe two biscuits on a small plate with a tall glass of milk that just whet your appetite for more. Now it's all you all the time, baby. Nobody is going to stop you except you. You can eat a whole row. **You can eat two whole rows.** You can plow them in there. You can savour them slowly. The point is it's such a great feeling to scoff biscuits with abandon like Cookie Monster.

Truly, he is the role model for us all.

AWESOME!

When a work friend becomes an outside-of-work friend

....

The nine-to-five brought you together.

Cracking jokes by the copier, **swapping stories on the line,** laughing in the lunchroom, you found a friend between policies, **procedures,** and paperwork. When you got together, you started noticing you were just you, **just hanging out,** just laughing about your day.

Then one day your friendship zoomed to a new level. Maybe you grabbed a beer one night, **got a surprise birthday invite,** or became new texting pals.

Yes, you turned a work friend into an outside-of-work friend, baby. It wasn't easy but you took the chance, **you made the leap,** and now you're rocking with someone new.

AWESOME!

Running to the door when your mum or dad comes home from work

....

After playing, playing, playing, you finally hear the car pull into the driveway, **the boots clomp up the steps,** and the key slide into the front door.

Time to drop what you're doing and race down the hallway for a big welcome back celebration.

Also known as The Hallway Rock Star Moment.

AWESOME!

Wearing a jumper that hasn't been washed yet

....

Feel that fuzz.

Yes, when you toss on a brand new jumper just smile and enjoy the smooth silky softness rubbing against your skin. There are no lint balls, **fraying sleeves**, or crinkled tags scratching at your neck. It's just the cottony soft freshness of a brand new friend.

Of course, we both know the washing machine and dryer will **slowly murder** our jumpers over time. That's why if you're like me you try and stretch out that cozy **first-wear feeling** as long as possible. You keep wearing it and wearing it **and wearing it** and wearing it, all the while hoping nobody calls you out on the fact that you don't wash your clothes.

But come on, it's worth it. It's worth the looks. It's worth the stares. It's worth the undershirts smeared with red lint. So go ahead! Toss on a pair of track pants, plop down on your cushy couch, and lie back in your sunny and relaxing world of

AWESOME!

Experiencing déjà vu

Déjà vu is that strange feeling of having already experienced a new situation sometime in the past. You chalk it up to a **dream or vision** of the future and briefly think you might be a long-lost descendant of Nostradamus who sees over the horizon of time. You conjure up visions of curing terrible diseases, **cashing in on the stock market**, or always getting the right answer on Final Jeopardy!

Now you just need to harness your powers.

AWESOME!

Tossing rubbish in the bin from far away

....

If your bad back, **busted ankle**, or bum knee is keeping you off the courts, then get ready to lean back and remember the game you loved . . .

Just grab the apple core, swivel your chair sideways, and shoot a majestic three-pointer into the metal rubbish bin. And don't worry—if you're inside the line, just go with a hook shot off the **glass fire extinguisher case** hanging on the wall.

Two points!

Now, before you start firing, it's important to make sure you've got a size and weight that works. Waxy, balled-up **hamburger wraps** are great. Flimsy granola bar wrappers are not. If you try tossing those granola bar wraps you'll find yourself missing the hoop and then casually glancing around to see who noticed before **sheepishly sharp-elbowing** your way to the rim to scoop your own dirty rebound.

No, the key to pulling it off is simple: Grab a ball that flies, **aim your hands to the skies**, and fire that rubbish into the bin nearby.

AWESOME!

Experiencing déjà vu

Déjà vu is that strange feeling of having already experienced a new situation sometime in the past. You chalk it up to a **dream or vision** of the future and briefly think you might be a long-lost descendant of Nostradamus who sees over the horizon of time. You conjure up visions of curing terrible diseases, **cashing in on the stock market**, and always getting the right answer on Final Jeopardy!

Now you just need to harness your powers.

AWESOME!

Taking your ponytail out

Okay, you know how good it feels when you peel your socks off at the end of the day? You know how your crinkly leg hairs all get a chance to relax, **stretch out**, and breathe a sigh of relief?

Well, taking out your ponytail is like that times a million.

All your hair unbends and finally points in the other direction. Shivers swirl down your spine as you curl your neck and shake your head out. Yes, all the pressure melts away and it feels like an **instant scalp massage**. Plus, if you tied your shaggy mane up when **it was wet,** then it's even better because somehow everything got twisted even tighter up in there. You can't wait to let it down and start scratching at that post-ponytail itchy scalp.

Taking your ponytail out is the **getting comfy** equivalent of putting on your PJs, taking your bra off at the end of the day, or twisting and turning all your sheets and blankets in the middle of the night till you get 'em *jusssssssssst* right.

AWESOME!

Learning a new keyboard shortcut

···

One day my friend Gillian told us about the first time **her mum** used a computer.

It was a long time ago, back, back, way back, and the story goes that the whole family was unpacking their **chunky new PC** in the middle of the lounge room. Styrofoam was cracked apart, boxes were torn up, and then they all slowly shuffled toward the grey **Box of the Future**, waiting for its information powers and **knowledge showers** to rain down upon them.

Now, most of the family had used a computer before so someone suggested mum get her **e-groove** on first. A lamp was turned on, a shiny wooden chair brought from the kitchen, and mum sat down while the machine slowly booted up. Then, while everybody was waiting, she carefully unwrapped the mouse from its plastic bag and calmly put it on the floor by her foot.

And as everybody watched, Gillian's mum slowly mimed typing and started pushing her foot on the mouse like **a sewing machine pedal**.

It was a hilariously cute moment.

Because we were all there once too.

Sure, maybe you didn't think stepping on the mouse made the computer go, but you probably were an awkward pile of **keyboard konfusion** as you got up to speed. Maybe you typed with two fingers or you took a tutorial to master double-clicking or signed up for DOS classes down at the city centre.

But come on, no matter what, no matter when, you know it's undeniably true: **You once sucked at computers too.**

But then you got a bit better, **then a bit better**, then a bit better, and now you're pretty good. You started double-clicking instead of triple-clicking, changed your resolution from super zoomed-in to super zoomed-out, and started typing without looking at the keys.

You turned into eYou, a barely recognisable quick-clicking Year 3000 cyborg version of yourself.

Of course, way down deep in your core you're still the same person who touched a computer for the first time and learned everything from scratch.

You still remember the excitement you felt as you learned all those tips and tricks. And that's what makes it exciting as you keep learning tips and tricks. Yes, whether it's a new keyboard shortcut or learning **how to whistle**, whether it's stopping on skates or playing "Stairway to Heaven" you still feel **the joy of learning** buzzing through your body every day.

You weren't sure if you could do it, but then you tried it, and then you could. You started CTRL+TAB'ing through your browser and CTRL+SHIFT+T'ing when your butterfingers accidentally closed a tab. You started Spacebarring

down websites and SHIFT+Spacebarring back up. You
CTRL-Z'd all your problems away, baby.

Learning a new keyboard shortcut feels great.

That's because learning anything new feels

AWESOME!

Figuring out a tricky plot twist just before they reveal it

....

Because at that moment you go from a greasy slack-jawed **popcorn-kernel-n-track-pants-covered** couch potato to a fast-talking screenwriter with sharp eyes, a whizzing mind, and a backup second career.

AWESOME!

Getting shotgun on a long car ride

We always brought quarters.

When I was younger someone's mum would always steer a **bumpy vanful** of us to the local shopping centre where we'd spend all Saturday watching movies, loitering in arcades, and flipping through crinkly video game magazines at 7-Eleven.

When we'd had our fill of action movies, **orange Slurpees**, and Street Fighter finishing moves, it was always time to **fish for quarters** and feed them into pay phones until someone's mum, dad, or big sister swung by to pick us up.

For years we were at the mercy of those drives to and from the shopping centre.

Sometimes they came, **sometimes they didn't**, sometimes we'd grab a taxi, sometimes we'd walk for kilometres through rain, kicking cigarette butts and tossing snowballs at stop signs.

Our world changed when we started getting our driver's licences.

Chad was first, then Mike, then the other Mike, then me, then Scott. Soon we were taking lessons, **practising with our parents**, and heading out in creaky cars, grabbing burgers, renting videos, and flipping through video game magazines at 7-Eleven.

Yes, we were a gangly pack of **sweaty sixteen-year-olds**, speeding on highways, smoking in car parks, and going on chicken wing crawls around town. They were dreamy days full of long laughs, wild thoughts, and big ideas. And I'll be honest when I tell you I miss them.

Of course, cramming into tight taxis with five other bony arses meant there were good seats and bad seats. Don't get me wrong: cruising through empty streets, **dark CBDs**, and flashing orange lights was always a fun time. But I'm just saying there were good seats and bad seats, that's all.

By far and away the best seat was **Shotgun**, also known as the passenger seat. To land this **Seat of Power**, adjusting radio stations, cranking air-conditioning, directing drivers, you simply had to yell out "Shotgun!," first, on the way to the car, within sight of the car. You got shotgun as many times as you could get it, as long as you called it, first, on the way to the car, within sight of the car.

By far and away the worst seat was **Hump**, also known as the middle seat in the back. To land this **Seat of Pain**, squeezed between pocket keys and pointy pelvises, straddling the floor bump, with only a thin lap belt holding you in, you simply had to yell out nothing, last, on the way to the car, within sight of the car. Generally there was some jockeying at that back door too, with overly polite grins and friendly hand gestures ushering you in, before you realised you were crawling headfirst into the alligator's mouth. Sometimes the score was ultimately settled through locked doors, **frantic racing around the car**, and dirty hip checks.

Since landing that middle seat was so painful my friends and I started yelling out "Anti-hump!" right after someone called shotgun. We agreed this move granted **Hump Immunity**, preventing the person who called it from getting saddled in that terrible seat, with its impossible-to-buckle-in-without-touching-someone's-arse seat belt.

When you got shotgun before a long drive you were loving it lots. You weren't responsible for eyes on the road and petrol in the tank. You weren't wedged into the sardine tin of sharp elbows and bony legs. No, you were **King of the Car**, Special Guest DJ, Emperor of Cold Air, and the most comfortable person on those long hauls to CBD concerts, distant cottages, or 7-Elevens way across town.

AWESOME!

That smooth feeling on your teeth after you get your braces off

···

Say goodbye to elastics, **say goodbye to nicknames**, say goodbye to closed-mouth-with-dimples smiles for family pictures.

When you finally get your braces off it's like being released from a **torture device** that has held you captive for years. Suddenly you can lick your front teeth, floss in less than an hour, and eat corn on the cob and **toffee apples** for dinner.

Welcome back, baby.

AWESOME!

That one email account you use for all your spam

Sorry, you need my email address?

Sure, no problem, clothing shop mailing list, **open-house real estate agent**, or random membership-required website.

Hit me up at idontcheckthisaccount@sorryaboutthat.com.

AWESOME!

Drawing on steamy mirrors with your fingers

Peel back that **mildewy curtain** and let's get down to business.

Freshly soaped and squeaky clean, your **wet n' steamy self** towels dry and rolls on some Stink-B-Gone deodorant. But just before you pop from the hot steam room to the **goose-bumpy hallway**, it's time to stop for a moment and be a finger-painting Picasso.

Yes, for a minute let the blurry morning haze and the upcoming stresses of school or work melt away as you start streaking your fingers up and down the steamy glass.

Crowds slowly gather at this **stormy seashore** and look over your shoulder as you calmly and quickly paint pretty pictures on your cliffside easel. Soon clouds part and the **sun glimmers** off the distant ocean waves as strangers stop walking their dogs, kids peek over from the ball diamond, and old folks hold hands and smile as you whip up masterpiece after masterpiece. Images pop up as they ooh and aah—it's a happy face, a heart, a house with smoke coming out the chimney, or a love letter waiting for the next person to have a shower.

Sure, in a few minutes the mirror fades to clear and your paintings drift away. But for an instant you're a **naked artist**, brushing up against greatness, fame, and a cluttery bathroom counter.

AWESOME!

Eating anything from your own garden

....

I was the Basil King.

A few summers ago I lived with a girlfriend in a cramped old apartment in the suburbs. The place didn't have an elevator or air-conditioning so we'd come home after some **sweaty staircase cardio** and strip off our shirts, flip on the fans, and eat icy poles on the balcony as sweat streamed down our shiny foreheads.

Dinner was always a quick affair with points awarded to whoever braved the **steaming hotbox** to whip up a meal without cranking the oven, turning on the stove, or moving very much.

Since we were spending most evenings sitting outside we decided to dress the balcony up a little bit. We upgraded our sticky plastic chairs to slippery nylon ones. We grabbed some **plastic tumblers** from the two-dollar shop. And, most important, we bought a tiny pot of basil and set it down in the corner.

It was the first garden I ever had.

And soon I loved that pot of basil like a son.

See, bouncing around uni sharehouses and basement apartments for years meant no time, no money, no gardens for me. The pot of basil was a new day, a new dawn, and a new life to look after. When we first sat it on the corner of that balcony, I looked down at it like it was a helpless new-born swaddled in rags in the delivery room.

"I will raise you like my own," I promised the tiny basil pot that day. "I will give you sunlight, I will give you water, I will give you love."

"I will eat your limbs," my girlfriend helpfully added, rubbing her belly and licking her lips like a **grizzly bear** gazing up at a sticky beehive in a tall pine tree.

But I meant my words and every day I'd poke around the plant, softly feeling the plastic sheen of new leaves, picking off tiny spiderwebs, and pouring clean water into its dirty home. Soon the basil rewarded me with **bright fragrant leaves** reaching up and out of its pot, trying desperately to give me a big hug for my love.

It wasn't long before everything we made included basil.

We threw it on pizzas, tossed it in pastas, and made enough pesto to open a flea market stand. I loved that plant like no other and it gave me a bountiful balcony harvest. We'd even freeze it in bunches and hand it out like loot bags to visiting friends. "Thanks for coming over," we'd say, stuffing a fat baggie into their hands and winking. "Here's a little something for the ride home."

It really is a beautiful moment eating anything from your own garden. In our modern world of pizza pockets,

meat pies, and canned everything, there's something real and something honest about raising your own plants. Forget pesticides, forget insect repellent, forget frozen fish sticks from the other side of the planet. This here's the real deal: planted out back, picked out back, and dropped straight into your dinner.

AWESOME!

Seeing shapes in the clouds

It's a genie coming out of a bottle, a big map of India, **a ballerina twirling on stage,** or . . .

AWESOME!

Long, comfortable silences
between really close friends

···

"Mmm, want the air-conditioning on or anything?"

"No, no, I'm good . . ."

AWESOME!

Going on a field trip in primary school

....

It all starts with the permission slip.

Yes, when teachers send them home before the bell rings so parents can rubber-stamp the **bumpy bus trip** to the museum, then it's on, my friends, **it's on.**

Soon the days count down and the buzz builds up as the class gets ready for the day away from school. The Middle Ages unit wraps up at **Medieval Times**, paintings are handed in before the art gallery, and everyone mails a friend a letter before the tour of the post office.

On the morning of the big day you wake up with some extra pep in your step because you know we're all heading away from school. It's time to skip the portables, **soggy sandwiches,** and long afternoons with the Spanish teacher.

It's time to do something different.

It's time to go for a ride.

Whether it's the petting zoo, **chocolate factory**, or a long hike in the woods, it's time to enjoy the school holiday with the following big perks:

1. **Subs in the house**. Taking thirty screaming seven-year-olds to the planetarium is a bit much, so most

teachers call in backups in the form of parent chaperones. These subs act like a sweet and jumpered army who don't know enough names or have enough power to mess up the fun. Of course, that's assuming they're not **your** mum or dad. If they are, your day is over.

2. **Wheels on the bus.** They go round and round on the way there and back. Yeah, we all gang-rush the slippery seat-belt-free seats and enjoy a loud, laughing party on wheels. There are loud, screechy songs, secret makeout sessions, and friendly gestures to passing motorists. This is also when the school social structure is on display—from the cool kids at the back to the awkward nerds sitting with the teacher up front. I really did love sitting up front, though, honestly. I mean, how about those big windows? What a view!

3. **Sealing it in.** A friend and I were strolling through an art gallery a couple of years back when we stumbled on a group of kindergartners holding a rope and looking at splotchy paintings. I'll never forget the jaw-dropping look of pure head-tilting amazement from the little boy at the end—eyes twinkling, mittens hanging out of his coat, his whirring brain soaking and swallowing something beautiful on the wall. And it's true: Field trips often help seal in the learning. Chalk one up for school.

So . . . let's enjoy the memories, **let's enjoy the moments**, and let's enjoy the car park speed bumps. Yes, let's all love those special days when **dusty blackboards** fade away and buses wheel us down the freeway . . . far away . . . far away . . . far away . . .

AWESOME!

The moment on a roller coaster when you get to the top of the big hill and before you go down it

You drive to the park, you walk to the gate, **you get your hand stamped**, you run to the line, you move up, you grab a hot dog, you move up, you check your watch, you get to the front, you jump in the ride, and then the big moment finally arrives: The screechy cars start moving, there's some **rumbly bumping**, and you're cranking up the big first hill and all you hear is chk, chk, chk, chk, chk, chk, chk, chk, chk.

Then there's a short, quiet pause as you teeter on the top and float for a brief second as the cars tip down, **your stomach twists around**, and your arms wave high as you get ready to scream.

AWESOME!

When that social event you didn't want to go to gets cancelled

....

Catch you next time, distant cousin's baby shower. We totally would have been there, new coworker's birthday party. Sorry it didn't work out, someone we don't know's wedding.

AWESOME!

Rocking out on air instruments

Oh, there's more than just guitar.

How many of these other air classics have you pulled off?

1. **Air Drums**. Riding shotgun and nailing solos on the dashboard or cooking dinner and feeling the beats on the kitchen bench, you either go with the My Fingers Are Drumsticks method or the My Fists Are Holding Air Drumsticks method. Both sound excellent.

2. **Air Keyboard**. No Air Résumé is complete without some strong Air Keyboard experience. Nail it by squeezing your eyes shut, raising your brows, biting your lip, and swaying back and forth.

3. **Air Harmonica**. Use sparingly for Bruce Springsteen and Tom Petty songs.

4. **Air Cowbell**. If you master Air Cowbell, be prepared to be invited to all the coolest parties and hottest dances. Bonus points for playing with a giant openmouthed smile and wildly bobbing head while being really, really tall.

Yes, rocking out in a state of air-playing bliss is one of life's great joys. When you're in the zone there's a **tear in the fabric of space-time** and you're suddenly transported to a sold-out Air Stage in front of millions and millions of sweaty screaming Air Fans.

Your big buckets of passion and neverending supply of energy help keep our planet spinning, so pump those fists, nail those high notes, and rock on, rock star, rock on.

AWESOME!

Doing anything that makes you feel like a caveman

There's something about getting in touch with your inner Neanderthal that strokes your brain stem just the right way. Accomplishing something caveman-style feels good—a combination of clenched teeth, throbbing veins, and good old fashioned feistiness that we don't always get to experience in today's sophisticated society.

Here are some things that deliver **a good cave high**:

- **Building a fire.** There's serious satisfaction to be had from collecting a pile of twigs and logs and sending them up in smoke. You're in the forest on your hands and knees, coaxing life-giving heat and energy out of dry, dead wood. For the full effect, leave the lighter fluid at home.

- **Eating a meal that is just meat.** Have you ever been that person at the buffet who loads their whole plate up with just meat? You know, slab of steak, couple of pork chops, maybe some ribs on the side? Sure, you see that potato salad, you see those steamed baby carrots, but you can't justify eating anything other than meat. Don't worry, your inner caveman thanks you. Bonus: filling your plate with drumsticks, chicken wings, and ribs so you can just eat messily off the bone with your bare hands.

- **Ignoring body hair for a really long time.** Your chin fuzz grows out and connects with your unkempt muttonchops, your hair gets long and scraggly, and you suddenly start getting Ch-Ch-Ch-Chia Back. This will keep you warm in the cave for winter.

- **Breaking something.** Maybe you're tossing an old dresser at the dump or splintering the broken-down shed for firewood. Either way, after you've delivered a few devastating boots, hammer swings, and stick smacks, make sure you let out a victorious roar to let the whole entire forest know you won the battle.

- **Throwing a temper tantrum much more aggressively than normal.** If you're the kind of classy gal who usually politely bee-beeps the horn when someone cuts you off, but then one time you hold it down for ten seconds, flip the bird, and scream out your window, then that's the one. That's your Beautiful Cavegirl Moment.

So I say love it. Love those caveman days, because they're a throwback to the simple life—when instead of eating processed cheese and watching reality TV we were clubbing sabre-toothed tigers and painting caves, baby.

AWESOME!

That teacher

....

Put your hand up if you ran from doorbells, **hid behind pant legs**, and avoided eye contact with grown-ups as a shy little kid.

Brothers and sisters, if your hand is up right now, you are not alone.

Yes, mute as a mouse, **quiet as a cat**, I was a short, snotty, bedhead-smeared ghost of a child until about eight years old.

That was when I was head-yanked out of my **turtle shell** by a cotton-white **curly-haired**, crinkly-smiled teacher who pushed me every single day. For some reason Mrs Dorsman cared, she just cared, and she had me reading to the class, talking out loud, and **practising my cursive** on the blackboard.

Sadly, when I was ten years old, my family moved away and we completely lost touch. But the little germs of ideas she planted in me rooted deep and grew slowly as the years bumped on and on and on and on . . .

Just after *The Book of Awesome* came out last year, I woke up and found this in my inbox:

From: Stella Dorsman
Neil, I just read an article in the paper this morning
about your interesting life and upcoming book. I just

need to know . . . are you the Neil Pasricha who was in my grade 3 class at Sunset Heights P.S.? If so, reading about you has been my truly awesome moment for today. I have been retired for ten years, but always remember my good students and hope that some of the emphasis I placed on writing skills eventually paid off. Please confirm your identity!

Best wishes,

Stella Dorsman

From: Neil Pasricha

It's me! It's me!

Mrs Dorsman, you did indeed inspire and encourage me. I remember our class fondly! You are a fantastic and passionate teacher and I'm sure you encouraged thousands of students in your career. I count myself amongst the lucky! Thank you for calling my name on your attendance list that cold morning after Labour Day.

Neil

From: Stella Dorsman

Neil, SO HAPPY to hear from you . . . and you're old enough to call me "Stella" now! I also remember your Sunset Heights class as one of the highlights of my career . . . not all classes were as much fun.

I will indeed check out your book . . . I'm very proud of you . . . Stella

Well, we've all got those teachers who plant seeds inside us. Maybe it's the **baseball coach** who leaves you on the mound after giving up some runs, maybe it's the language teacher who helps you with that stutter after class, or maybe it's the college professor whose **inspirational talks** fill you with the power to follow your dreams.

Mrs Dorsman ended up coming to the book launch for *The Book of Awesome*, where she joined me onstage and took the mic and told stories from decades ago to hundreds of people. After she spoke I gave her a big hug and a signed book . . . and told her to check out the Acknowledgments buried deep in the back where every single copy has a tiny little note waiting there just for her.

"Special thanks to Mrs Dorsman for pushing me out of my shell in third grade."

AWESOME!

When somebody holds the elevator door for you

Close Door people, we see you.

Don't pretend you don't know what we're talking about. We see you duck into the elevator twenty steps before us in the lobby and tap-tap-tap that **Close Door** button so you can score a slightly faster ride. What, you think we don't notice your attempts to avoid eye contact? Oh, we do, and we don't like you for it either.

No, the people we like are a different sort of people. They're **Open Door** people. They're the ones with the bruises on their forearms, tapping the Open button, and popping their head out to ask innocently, **"Going up?"**

Why yes, we are going up. Why yes, we would love to share the lift with you. Why yes, we'll smile and thank you for holding it. And why yes, we'll keep it open when we see you coming the next time too.

Now let's all hug and chug-a-lug home.

AWESOME!

Setting the new high score on a video game

....

It's a big deal.

When I was a little kid my friends and I took pictures of the TV screen after setting new high scores. It was so important to us we'd even mail the photos to video game magazines hoping they'd splash them across their pages as a late-breaking scoop.

Two eight-year-olds defeat Bowser in epic battle
No-holds-barred cave fight features
fireballs and flying hammers

Yes, if you've been there you know the road to setting a new high score is paved with lots of swearing, **tossed controllers,** and empty cans of soft drink. Blurry eyes, all-day bedhead, and slowly expanding pit stains are the mark of these basement-dwelling champions.

Now, while cracking top spot at home offers a big rush, there's something to be said about the **rare moment** you actually pull it off in an old arcade.

After all, you probably dumped a few buckets of quarters into the machine just to get to **M. Bison,** so the payoff was your treat for spending weeks of allowance and lolly money. Also, you got to put your initials into the machine, which means you can go with your actual initials, the **AAA default**, or the filthiest three-letter word you know. Just make sure nobody unplugs the machine, and have a couple of witnesses so you've got proof of being *the* A.S.S. at Tony's Pizza Slice who racked up 171,000 points on **Ms Pac-Man**.

Setting a new high score on a video game is a moment of total euphoria. Your heart speeds up and your brain flies off as you realise you're making it big. Yes, you turned tightly on **Rainbow Road**, nailed a Tetris when the screen was full, and hit all the right notes on the guitar.

The blisters, eyestrain, and malnutrition were worth it, you think to yourself, as you survey your dark and seedy den of empty chip bags, **greasy pizza boxes**, and dirty socks. And as that slow smile curls across your face make sure you take a long, quiet moment to stare at the TV screen and bask in your glowing moment of guts and glory.

AWESOME!

Taking a spin on a
shopping trolley

....

Hey, baby.

Take a ride on the wild side.

Yes, while walking down that **empty supermarket** aisle look left at the Cocoa Puffs, look right at the rice cakes, nod confidently, and then step on the trolley and fly.

Apples bounce, **bread slides**, and there are some intense g-forces on your salami. But a few seconds later, a few feet away, how much are you smiling after that dangerous **floor-tile thrill ride** to the yoghurt?

Now, there are a few different ways the dangerous deeds go down. Here we go:

1. **Pedal to the Metal**. This is the classic one-foot ride to heaven. Two hands on the bar, one foot jammed underneath, and your back leg hanging out like a wobbly figure skater. Just make sure you've got a watermelon and a sack of potatoes in your trolley to hold her steady.

2. **Two-Footer**. This is the Pedal to the Metal with more commitment. Without your skiddy-soled runners providing an emergency brake, anything could

happen. Remember to know your limits and play it safe out there.

3. **A-Tisket, A-Tasket.** Someone's riding in the basket. Make sure you don't crash into a wall of soup, because the only air bags in this thing are full of onions.

4. **The Station Wagon.** Remember that backseat in old station wagons facing the opposite direction? This is the shopping trolley version. Hold on tight to the front of the trolley and cross your fingers the driver doesn't steer you into the egg wall.

5. **The Submarine.** Highly not recommended. This deep-sea move consists of riding underneath where the soft drink cans and nappies usually sit. It also consists of being at the mercy of the lunatic driver above you. Remember to be safe in that supermarket jungle. Nobody wants to go home with a forehead full of kidney bean can dents.

Yes, taking a quick spin on a shopping trolley is a coffee aisle holiday.

It's juice and jam jubilation.

It's a nappy dash temptation.

And it's a supermarket celebration.

AWESOME!

Slurping hot soup on
a cold night

....

Say it's a cold, bone-shivering night.

Say there's snow shooting sharp, **shooting sideways,** shooting into your eyes, and the wind is just howling and twirling into mini-tornadoes, slicing and dicing deep through your coat and into your chest. Your fingers are icicles, your nose a **dented, frozen strawberry,** and your cheeks look like someone ran them over with a cheese grater a few times.

On nights like this, just face it: **You're an ice-cold mess.**

You need to get home fast and eat some soup.

Yes, you need to stomp your boots, shake the snow off your jacket, let your glasses steam up, and touch-feel your way to the kitchen to heat it up, pour it up, **snag those saltines up,** and sit right down to slurp up one of life's great pleasures:

- **Temperature check.** That soup's steaming hot and you're ice cold and now is not the time for First-Degree Tongue Burn. Make sure your slurps force cooler air into your mouth to chill the soup out a bit. It's like cooling beer bottles in the freezer for a few minutes or nuking the cold half of your dinner for ten seconds to heat it back up—just some temperature knob twiddling to get it *jusssssst* right.

- **Our ancestors did it.** What, do you think cavemen sipped their soup politely? No, I bet they slurped it straight from the sabre-tooth skull and loved doing it. Next time your date pops up from her steak with gravy on her cheeks, **meat in her teeth**, and mashed potato in her hair, just flash a big thumbs-up and start slurping your soup. It's all about embracing our common roots.
- **Get closer.** To slurp properly, you may need to hunch right on over the soup bowl. Yes, lean those shoulders forward and let that steam fog up your glasses and thaw your face. You are a few centimetres closer to being at one with the soup. It's your Chicken Noodle Moment of Zen.

So next time you get home from a long and cold walk home, just heat up some soup and start laying down some **wet and juicy slurps**.

Also works with hot chocolate.

AWESOME!

Turning off all the lights during a thunderstorm

Hey, it's not like you can play outside, **go swimming**, ride your bike, or walk to the shop. So just flick off the lights, yank open the blinds, and stare out the window at the majestic streaks of bright lightning cracking down all around you.

AWESOME!

The Perfect Egg Crack

....

Put your hand up if you've ever tried to fish out some **slippery, slathery** eggshell pieces from a bowl full of raw egg.

Brother, I been there too and we both know it ain't pretty. **Shell Diving** sure is high on the **Kitchen Humiliation List**, together with dropping a piece of toast jam-side-down, opening the oven door and having massive black clouds blow out, or cracking an ice cube tray so strongly you send rogue cubes scattering across the floor.

Yes, The **Awful Egg Crack** is guaranteed to redden cheeks and knock amateur chefs down a few pegs, so that's why it's sweet when you finally master The Perfect Egg Crack. You can do it at home, by yourself, with a bit of practice. Just follow these three easy steps:

> **Step 1. The Tap N' Crack.** There is some debate on where exactly the egg should be tapped. Most folks like to tap the egg against an edge, like the side of a mixing bowl, but some argue you should only tap the egg against a flat surface, like a kitchen bench or cutting board. Whatever you choose, just be sure to only dent the shell lightly instead of giving it a career-ending stab wound.

Pushing too hard will result in a **Slime Explosion**, which isn't good unless you want to be called **Salmonella Hands** for the rest of your life.

Step 2. Big Thumbs. This is the moment of truth. Stick your two thumbs in the dent and in one swift move dig them in deep and pull them apart. If you did it right, the shell should snap easily into two beautiful pieces, dropping its slippery plunder into the bowl below. Now, some people opt for the One-Handed Move instead of ol' faithful Big Thumbs, but I say that's too risky. Besides, what are you really going to do with that free hand anyway?

Step 3. The Inspection. Go ahead, give it a once-over. Grab a magnifying glass or hold it up to the light if you need to. But I'm going to guess it's looking pretty pretty, my friend because you just performed a Perfect Egg Crack.

Beat that egg, fry that egg, whip that egg into cake batter. It's time to say goodbye to Kitchen Humiliation and hello to some well-deserved Kitchen Pride.

AWESOME!

Curling up into the fetal position

....

Girl, you used to fit in a shoe box.

Back when you were **all nude, all the time**, you were crunched up real fine in your mum's tum. Yes, your head was bowed down, your back was bent forward, your legs were pulled to your chest, and everything was in order.

The fetal position is the medical term used to describe your **Totally Comfy Pre-Born Position**. You're all curled up into a comfy little ball in there and while mum may notice you rattling around a bit, you're actually pretty chilled out and relaxed.

I mean, there's a reason **La-Z-Boy** doesn't make a womb-sized version, and brother, it ain't because they can't. No, it's because there's just no demand. Pre-born babies are already living the life of leisure and no amount of built-in cup holders, pillowy-soft headrests, or **swing-out footrests** can improve that.

Now, the fetal position has many **post-pop** uses as well.

First of all, some people sleep this way after they're born. They find it a safe and comfy way to ferry into **Dreamland** each evening. And this isn't just hearsay, people. Yes, I used to be a fetal position junkie myself as a kid, sleeping on my side like a **pyjama-clad jelly roll**.

Secondly, what's up with all those **bears**? Studies suggest that playing dead in the fetal position is a good strategy to ward off further pawing from friendly grizzlies in the forest.

Lastly, it just feels like home. The fetal position is the best way to keep warm if you find yourself **tentless in Greenland** or crashing on a pal's basement floor without copious blanketing. It literally warms the heart (liver, lungs, and kidneys).

And hey, isn't the fetal position just one more way to turn back the clock? After all, your body **knows** the fetal position, your body **lived** the fetal position, and so when you're trying to catch a few z's on the cold floor of a bear-infested forest, I think you know what to do.

Curl right up, baby.

For me and you.

AWESOME!

Old, classic board games

Wedged tightly into dark corners in dusty attics are piles of worn-out board games from years ago.

The corners of these old boxes are cracked and split open and the flashy prints on top long worn away, leaving only the dusty, corrugated bones behind. **Pencils with broken leads**, yellowed instructions, faded homemade scorecards, and assorted sub-ins for lost game pieces litter the box and make it look like a clattery **junk drawer** of assorted knickknacks. Take a deep breath and sniff up that musty scent that takes you way, way back.

For old times' sake, let's look fondly at ten of the greatest board games of all time:

10. **Mouse Trap**. This game taught us the meaning of the slow, tantric crescendo. That's because the first 99 per cent of the game was a boring, play-by-numbers hopscotch. But then it got to mouse trap time, and it was *alllllllll* worth it.

9. **Connect Four**. Despite the quick setup time, easy rules, and fun gameplay, Connect Four always seemed suspiciously mathy. And now, be honest—did you ever realise your kid sister was about to

deliver a four-in-a-row knockout punch and then release the trap on the bottom, spilling all the pieces on the table and denying her that big crowning moment? Hey, I'm not proud of it either.

8. **Battleship.** The best part of Battleship was those hard, plastic cases the game came in. It was like its own luggage set and it was hard not to feel important when you flipped one open and began fiddling with all the pieces inside. Kids, those are what we used to call laptops.

7. **Uno.** Now, Uno wasn't really a board game, but whenever it was Board Game Time there was always that one whiny kid who begged everyone to play Uno instead. But no one would. That's why it's called Uno.

6. **Risk.** Turns out you can't dominate the world in an hour. As a result, committing to a game of Risk was committing to giving up your entire evening. Games could go until three, four, five in the morning, with the first person out at 9 p.m. sitting bored on the couch flipping channels for six hours. Too bad, man. Shouldn't have challenged Siam.

5. **Candyland.** This game required no reading, no writing, no strategy, and no decision making at all. You just flipped over a card, looked at the colour, and moved your piece to that colour. That's it,

really. Candyland ranks high because it's a gateway game and gets people interested in the harder stuff.

4. **Trivial Pursuit.** The hardest stuff of all. I'm talking about the original, heavy-box Genus Edition here. You know you're playing that one when the questions are impossible and everybody feels like an idiot without any pie pieces. Props to the first person who proposes ditching the board and just asking questions.

3. **The Game of Life.** If you can believe it, Milton Bradley himself created The Game of Life way back in 1860. Now, the game is more than a little preachy—I mean, if you don't go to university, have lots of kids, and drive around buying insurance and suing for damages, then you probably won't be able to end up in a beautiful white plastic mansion at the end. But there was something special about all the kids getting to act grown up for an hour.

2. **Cluedo.** This dark and bloody board game about mansion murder was always a winner with happy-go-lucky kids on Saturday afternoons. Yes, Cluedo was a tense and quiet hour of private note taking, raised eyebrows, and suspicious glances. A nice break from running around the backyard with untied shoelaces and runny noses anyway.

1. **Monopoly.** After everyone is through fighting over the Free Parking rules and who gets the best token, this game was usually all about the late-inning **game-changing trade**. It's the three-way deal that gives the richest player all the railroads to seal everybody's fate or the tired person who gives up at midnight and just trades away Boardwalk to meet the rent on Kentucky Ave.

Yes, as you are huddled around the **kitchen table**, sitting in a friend's basement late at night, or gathering the family together at the cottage, there's just something about those old, classic board games. They sure do bring us together for some laughs, some ups, some downs, and some plain old fashioned gooooooooood times.

AWESOME!

When the bubbles in your drink go right to the top but not over

Pouring a **cold soft drink** or jug of beer can be stressful.

Yes, all eyes are watching as you attempt a **Hot Spotlight Pour** late at night, surrounded by thirsty people, empty glasses, and focused, judging eyes.

You could get sloppy and cause a **Bubbly Volcano** to erupt, staring in horror as the drink owner tries to quickly suck up all the carbonated lava spilling over the edge of the glass. Most likely, you'll end up with sticky hands, a wet table, and some nasty **stinkeye**.

Or you could have the opposite problem and pour a **Coke No Show**. That's when you cut your pour off early because you're afraid of the Volcano, but when the **Coke fizz** or **beer head** settles down and leaves only half a glass, well—that's just embarrassing.

No, the perfect situation is when you pour a drink where the bubbles go right to the top **but don't spill over**. It's an exhilarating rush to see those bubbles just fizz **up and up and up and up** to the top, and then a massive wave of relief when they calm right back down just in the nick of time.

AWESOME!

When your ears pop back to normal after swimming

....

Do you sometimes forget your ears need popping?

After the jet cabin decompresses, **concert wraps up**, or swimming lessons finish, the volume in your ear dials down a couple of notches and your head feels plugged up. But you get used to it. You pick up your baggage, clear customs, **jump on the subway**, towel off, get changed, and life keeps go— THEN SUDDENLY YOUR EARS POP AND EVERY- THING IS REALLY LOUD AND BACK TO NORMAL AGAIN.

AWESOME!

That old Take a Penny, Leave a Penny bowl on the shop counter

....

Nobody likes pennies.

Sure, maybe in the 1800s they scored you a handful of gumballs or the evening edition of your local *Times-Express*, but these days they're barely worth 1 per cent of a **Snickers** bar. Go on, lick the edge of a Snickers and scrape off a few chocolate molecules with your tongue. That, that right there, that's a penny.

Now, having said that, there's one moment where the value of a penny shoots sky-high, and that's when the beef jerky and **energy drink** at the petrol station rings up to $8.01. If you're cringing right now it's because you know that's a terrible price, leading to a few Checkout Possibilities:

1. **By the Rules.** One option is just to roll with it. Break that ten and get ready for a mittful of change, including the dreaded **Four-Penny Punch-out**. Now your pocket is busting and your hand smells like dirty copper, but what are you going to do? You played by the rules and you lost.

2. **The Cashier Cheat**. You can never predict when this happens. Sometimes you're expecting to play by the rules, but the cashier just rounds up or down for you. When Bill-Counting Betty doesn't care about the till balance, she just drops you some loose change and a wink.

3. **The Bowl**. Finally, the feature attraction. Since you don't want ninety-nine cents jingle-jangling around your pocket, you eye the Take a Penny, Leave a Penny bowl and see what's shaking. You've made your deposits over the years, so don't feel guilty about a little withdrawal now.

Yes, the Take a Penny, Leave a Penny bowl brings out the best in us. It's a stranger-to-stranger donation that pays you back after you pay it forward. Just remember: Take a penny, leave a penny?

Take a favour.

Leave a legacy.

AWESOME!

When someone saves you a seat

It's time to get down with the get down . . .

At the movies! Your arms bearhug fat tubs of popcorn and slippery jumbo drinks as you blindly stumble down the dark aisle. You scan the chattery crowd dotting the red plushy tundra before noticing your friend thirty rows up giving you the two-armed wave.

At the school assembly! You're separated from your fourth-grade soul mate and only see each other while double-dutching by the portables at recess. But then come student council speeches, music recitals, or a Thanksgiving play and suddenly your hearts spark again at the back of the bleachers.

At the concert! Boots up, you're bumpily crowdsurfing at the front of the mosh pit. After you crashland on your neck in a dirty puddle of warm beer, your friend yanks you up by the wrist and squeezes you beside her right in front of the stage.

At the rocket ship before blastoff! You slept in and got stuck in highway traffic so now you're chomping on a fistful of ice cream pellets while Velcroing your aluminum-foil-and-fishbowl getup together in the car. You arrive at the launch-pad and race down the thin metal bridges into the ship as the engines fire up . . . and there's Cindy! With a jumper lying on the window seat beside her.

Yes, when you spot a friend snagging you a **prime seat** it's good times, it's good times. After all, they're expressing your friendship **to the world** by deciding twenty minutes of stink-eye is worth making sure you sit together.

AWESOME!

The sound of water lapping against a dock

It sounds like the **warm and windy** start of summer. It sounds like the cool and quiet finish to autumn.

AWESOME!

When the delivery food you ordered somehow arrives really early

....

Grumbling tums make those late snacks come every time.

Scope this scene:

It's late at night, **clock clicking** past two in the morning, and you and your friends are lying on a torn, potato-chip-crumb-covered couch, sporting big grins, slack jaws, droopy eyes, and **sweaty T-shirts.** You're half awake but fully hungry, half cooked but not fully done, half exhausted but fully up for ordering some **hot and steamy late night food.**

Someone suggests it and everybody wants it. And then it's all over.

First you start picturing **burning hot mozzarella** sliding around on slippery tomato sauce. You think of wet and glistening pepperoni, the corners black and crispy, little **grease puddles** lying in the folds. Then you start dreaming of steamy Styrofoam with sticky sweet-and-sour chicken. Then you're salivating over thought bubbles of greasy samosas and pillowy naans in paper bags. And you know, you just know, that late night food will taste delicious. Because how can it not?

See, we all know this ain't your **6 p.m. Dinner Order**, where opinions are collected, phone numbers are looked up, and the table is set for dinner, complete with triangle-folded paper towels and a giant **2-litre bottle of Coke** centrepiece.

No, this is the **Late Night Scoff-It-And-Sleep**. This is the one your doctor warned you about. This is the one that took out Grandpa. Yeah, this is the big ball of greasy grub that sponges up everything else in your belly. It's the only cure for rapid outbreaks of the **Midnight Munchies**, that empty, raw, growling feeling your gut gives you when it's tired and confused and suddenly wants breakfast.

The Scoff-It-And-Sleep generally consists of somebody dialing whatever number is in their mobile phone, ordering a **plain cheese or pepperoni pizza** or random Mixed-Plate Combo #6 without asking anybody else, and then just throwing it on their credit card because they can't be bothered to collect five bucks from everybody sitting around playing video games.

The only issue with the Scoff-It-And-Sleep is that even in the middle of the night you get told what you always get told: "That'll be forty-five minutes," they say. And brother, you know and I know that you don't want to be waiting for that food, that long, that late. Somebody might crack and **drink a bottle of salad dressing** or eat a bar of butter, man. It's a tense scene.

And that's why it's great when, once in a while, you get that surprise really, really early delivery. When twelve minutes after you place your order, the doorbell rings and **wham-bam, thank you gram**, it's here, it's hot, and it's time to toss that greasy square of hot cardboard on the floor or big stapled paper bag on the bench and rip right into it like a pack of lions around a **dead zebra**.

So this one goes out to the delivery people who surprise us with an early doorbell once in a while. Thanks for filling our bellies with your **greasy goodness** just in time for bed.

AWESOME!

Acrobatic snoozing

Everybody loves a good snooze.

That's where you groggily dive back into the sleepy underworld for a few more minutes of **lazy-boned bliss** before waking up to get your day on. It's even better when you tap the snooze button with a bit of acrobatic showmanship that keeps you dreaming before your **wide-awake self** invades your space.

Here's how to keep on snoozing in the free world:

1. **The Blindfold.** You've long memorised the shape and location of your snooze button, so when it starts buzzing you don't even open your eyes. Nope, you just fumble until you find it and kick back for nine more minutes of heaven.

2. **The Behind The Back.** Here's where you're facing away from the alarm clock when it starts ringing, but instead of flipping right over you casually toss your arm in the air and reach backwards until you find the snooze. Also known as the Reverse Angle Shoulder Twist.

3. **The Outsource.** Perhaps your clock starts buzzing as your boyfriend is hopping around putting pants on

or while your sister's knocking to wake you up. Either way, you outsource your snoozing to them with a cute and groggy "Mmmnnn . . . can you hit . . . button."

4. **The Toe Tap.** You've been tossing and turning all night and now you've got the Toe Vent going in a perfect spot to use your foot to tap the button. If you manage to avoid knocking over your glass of water or accidentally kicking your alarm clock to the floor, this can be a stunningly beautiful move.

Yes, pulling off an acrobatic snooze makes you feel like a **trapeze artist** way up inside a big tent at the roaring climax of the circus. Sweat drips down your forehead and onto your **tight white unitard** as you stare with steady eyes at your wide-eyed partner swinging toward you. Suddenly you bend your knees and **jump high and wide** into their open arms before quickly locking and soaring breathless over all the bright lights below . . .

Elephants trumpet, **lions roar**, and jaws drop as you somersault with a smile way, way up in the darkness. The ringmaster points his cane at you and screams while thundering applause rains down.

So snooze for the moment. Snooze for the memories.

Snooze for your life.

AWESOME!

Doing your first headstand

....

Pull the floor mat to the wall and let's get down to business. Yes, it's time to flip yourself up and fall back down in an **awkward crumbling somersault** of knees and elbows. After crashing on your first dozen tries you eventually find yourself teetering for a second, wobbling clumsily, and then quickly steadying yourself so you're perfectly upside down.

You're doing your first headstand.

AWESOME!

Eating foods you loved
as a kid

....

The flood of memories that comes shooting back when you eat food you loved as a kid is a giant, neuron-splattering head rush. You're suddenly transported back to the kitchen you grew up in and can practically see the avocado-green stove, three-hundred-kilo microwave, and plastic alphabet magnets covering the fridge.

So come on, let's all go back:

- **Squished-up balls of fresh bread.** This one involves taking a piece of really soft, really fresh bread, ripping off all the crusts, and then rolling it into a tight, white ball of dense deliciousness. Feel free to hide a wedge of butter in the core there too.
- **Whatever you ate for holiday meals.** Maybe back at The Kids Table you were loving Grandma's pumpkin pie, your brother's lumpy mashed potatoes, or mum's famous stuffing. Nothing tastes as good when the holidays hit.
- **Boxed macaroni with chopped-up hot dogs.** Stare into that hot steamy fluorescent orange bowl and get ready to chow down. Optional features include add-

ing massive squirts of tomato sauce or chopped-up hot dogs. Not optional is eating the whole box.

- **Tang.** The beautiful thing about Tang is that as you get older, you can just water it down a bit if you can't handle the sweetness anymore. Or you can do the opposite and have yourself a glass of Super Tang. After that, it's time to blast off to the moon.

- **Melted Cheese.** This is one that my sister and I used to love. We would put a piece of bread on a plate, slice up five thin slices of cheese, and then nuke it for thirty seconds. We had it down to an exact science. Once in a while things would get a little crazy and we'd put some tomato sauce on it, but mostly just Melted Cheese. A perfect name for a perfect after-school snack.

- **Liquid antibiotics.** Okay, it's not really a food, but how about that sugary amoxicillin you used to get? You can apparently still ask for it as an adult, but you might need to take eight teaspoons fourteen times a day to get your full dosage.

- **Those cheese spread cracker kits with the red plastic stick.** Who else always ran out of cheese way before they ran out of cracker?

- **Your favourite sandwich.** Maybe today you're on a health kick, but remember when your favourite sandwich was bologna and processed cheese on white bread? Or salami and mustard and mayo?

Or creamy peanut butter with grape jam cut into triangles?

- **Canned pasta.** Whether your fancy is beef ravioli or the tangy sweetness from a soupy bowl of tomato-sauce-soaked O's, these piles of sodium and meatpaste definitely tickle the memory bone.

- **Mum's Spaghetti Sauce.** Was your mum a jar of sauce in a pot kind of gal? Or a slow, all-day simmering type of lady? Did she leave the mushrooms chunky, chop them real fine, or leave them out completely? What was her position on onions, melted cheese on top, or meatballs versus meat sauce? If you grew up with homemade spaghetti sauce, I'm willing to bet it's still something that tastes amazing today.

- **Cold hot dogs straight from the fridge.** Oh, don't worry. The worms all died in the factory.

- **Random mishmash desserts.** My sister used to put oats and butter in the microwave and top it with a spoon of brown sugar. Maybe you loved Milo on a spoon, butter and sugar sandwiches, homemade Coke ice pops, or Nutella smeared on anything.

- **Sugar cereals.** I ate Corn Pops every day for breakfast for a decade and somehow survived. These days, you can always cut them with an adult cereal if they're too sweet. Throw some plain Cheerios on those Honey Nut Cheerios or some Corn Flakes on those Frosted Flakes. Just don't tell anybody, old man.

Now, let's be honest, sometimes the foods you loved as a kid slowly drift away and disappear. Grandma passes on and her **secret meatball recipe** is buried with her, you move away from the sibling you used to bake your special Christmas slice with, or the sugar in your sugary cereal suddenly turns into a more profitable fructose chemical spray.

But that's why it's doubly important to treasure those adult glimpses into your childhood tastes. That's why you gotta love those perfect little loves at first bite. That's why the **memory jolts** from the sugary treats and salty snacks are such amazing little highs. Because even though your stomach may not always thank you for it, your brain surely will.

AWESOME!

Calling a mulligan on the day

Do you play golf?

Me, I've tried a couple of times but it's always the same: I lace up some stained sneakers, borrow **rusty clubs** from someone's basement, and then scrounge around the car park for some tees for my once-a-decade tee shot.

Now, I've got absolutely no athletic abilities so you'll understand why I love that golf rule that lets me **call a mulligan.** Have you heard of it? Basically, I swing and miss the ball a dozen times before eventually shanking it **dead sideways** into the dense forest.

But then I just yell **MULLIGANNNNN!** really loudly and everyone lets me try again.

It's a great rule and it got me thinking: We should be able to call mulligans anywhere.

Because hear me out.

What if you could call a mulligan on your driving test? Yes, after tyre-punching the curb and **hitting Grandma's shopping trolley,** you just drop the m-word and start again. Or how about calling a mulligan after an **awkward goodbye kiss** in the airport? Or after accidentally spitting a **tiny piece of food** on your date's face?

It's starting to sound good, am I right?

My old uni friend Mike is the absolute master. See, he's perfected the beautifully indulgent **Weekend Mulligan**. He often gets up and groggily stumbles around the kitchen, spills coffee grinds on the floor, and accidentally steps on the cat. But then he stares at his **dark, hollow eyes** in the mirror and realises he woke up too soon.

That's when he just **calls a mulligan on the day** and goes back to bed with a plan to give it another shot a few hours later.

People, life's too short not to sleep when you feel like it so take a page from our book and when your first couple of tries land in the rough, just yell mulligan and start again.

We all deserve a second chance.

AWESOME!

Finally getting the perfect picture

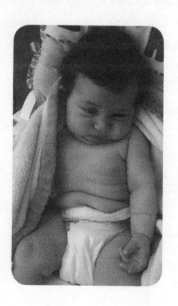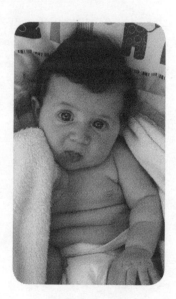

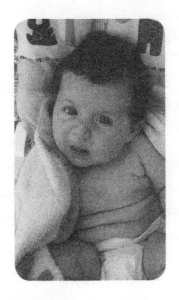
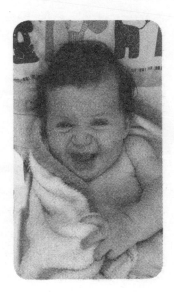

AWESOME!

Fat baseball players

If you ever find yourself playing professional sports and someone from the stands yells out, "Come on, Big Bopper!" you're probably a fat baseball player. Fat baseball player, thank you for giving us that simplest thing of all.

Hope.

See, because usually when we see those **tricep flabs** shaking in the wind and those bathroom scales exploding into a mess of springs going in all directions, we figure that our professional sports careers are pretty much over. Ain't too much room on the ice hockey bench or the soccer pitch for us husky folks, and so, with our dreams sidelined, we sign up for night school **VCR repair courses** and start staining furniture in the garage, channeling our energies away from the games we love into our Plan Bs and Cs.

But that's where you come in. To the chunky outfielders, chubby pinch hitters, and doughy-arsed relief pitchers of the world: Thank you for keeping our dreams alive to one day be a platoon Designated Hitter. Thank you for being

AWESOME!

Watching something download really fast

The first website I ever visited was **Yahoo.com**.

The whole sordid affair went down in the mid-nineties on a school trip to the **Science Centre**. While other kids from our class learned how paper was made or watched **3D films** about the Amazon, my friends and I raced to a dim room at the back stuffed with clunky computer monitors sitting in a big circle. See, we had read ads in the paper about a new exhibit showcasing the new **Informative Superb Highway** and we wanted to experience the straight dope firsthand.

Unfortunately for us, someone tipped off all the geeks from other schools too and the room was jam-packed with sweaty nerds in long lines waiting for small **ten-minute turns** to ride the wave.

Well, we waited and waited and waited and eventually scored a yellow plastic stool in front of a big screen. Giddy as schoolgirls, we decided to begin **expanding our minds** and broadening our horizons by researching the hit TV show *Baywatch*. See, we had many questions about the complex plot of this show, which required detailed investigation.

Now remember—this was the mid-nineties here. Mobile phones looked like briefcases, encyclopedias filled home libraries, and young kids with dirty faces stood on street-corner **soapboxes** hawking evening editions of the local *Times-Express* on your way home from work.

In these dark times, the only website any of us had heard of was **Yahoo.com**, so after spending a few minutes finding and opening the browser, we typed in the website, pressed Enter, and began waiting for this new **dawn of civilisation** to pour down on our young and eager heads.

But first . . .

. . .

. . .

. . . there was nothing.

Just a blank screen in a dim room filled with nerves, **teen sweat**, and yellow plastic stools. We waited and prayed until eventually **heart-pounding teasers** dribbled out at the bottom of the screen. **"Contacting server,"** it pledged, which sounded promising until it updated itself with only **"Connecting to server"** a minute later. Then a couple more minutes and "Transferring data" finally began and big red pixels slowly dropped into view.

But it was too late.

Our time was finishing up.

Yes, our big dreams and wild ideas of exploring this **magical fantasyland** on the other end of the wires dissolved into a page full of text, broken links, and a complete lack of swimsuits.

We walked away that day brokenhearted.

Some of us cried.

But now, way up here in the future, when I look back on that long bus ride home, **I smile** at how far we've come. These days websites load in the blink of an eye and songs zip home in seconds. As those little bar graphs fill up, we rub our palms together and cackle like madmen because now we never have to wait before watching videos of dancing cats and skateboarding accidents.

AWESOME!

A really cold drink on a really hot day

....

When your eyes sting from big salty beads of dripping sweat, your T-shirt gets wet and melts to your back, and your upper lip forms a **splotchy sweatstache**, then I say brother, it's time for a drink.

If you're feeling this heat then you know nothing says **refreshing** better than a **soaking wet can of soft drink** pulled from the icy depths of a giant picnic cooler, **wet frosty mug of cold beer** at the back of a dark bar, or tall condensation-covered glass of ice-cold water.

I mean, when you chug that stuff down it feels like **swallowing an icicle**. You can actually feel that cold river tearing down the chute and coating your insides. You can feel your throat pulsing, your stomach clenching, and your entire body drop a couple of degrees.

Drinking a really cold drink on a really hot day is a refreshing moment of chilly bliss that feels so incredibly
AWESOME!

Seeing old people holding hands

....

It's what life's all about.

Seeing old people holding hands is a symbol of a **lifelong companionship** full of knowing glances, **inside smiles**, and warm feelings in waiting hearts. As you watch them mosey down the boardwalk during the sunset you can't help see the connection of two hands that helped shape the world. Those hands made meals, **held babies**, mowed lawns, and fixed cars. They held faces, went places, called friends, and touched stars.

They tried and built and grew together. They lived and learned and loved together.

Seeing old people holding hands is a simple expression of **long lasting affection** that fills our hearts with hope. They show us a future world exists of tied-together hearts and **long lives lived** with someone we love.

AWESOME!

Seeing a really happy dog out for a walk

I'M OUTSIDE! I'M OUTSIDE! I'M OUTSIDE! I'M OUTSIDE! I'M OUTSIDE!
I'M OUTSIDE! I'M OUTSIDE! I'M OUTSIDE! I'M OUTSIDE! I'M OUTSIDE!
I'M OUTSIDE! I'M OUTSIDE! I'M OUTSIDE! I'M OUTSIDE! I'M OUTSIDE!
I'M OUTSIDE! I'M OUTSIDE! I'M OUTSIDE! I'M OUTSIDE! I'M OUTSIDE!
I'M OUTSIDE! I'M OUTSIDE! I'M OUTSIDE! I'M OUTSIDE! I'M OUTSIDE!
I'M OUTSIDE! I'M OUTSIDE! I'M OUTSIDE! I'M OUTSIDE! I'M OUTSIDE!

AWESOME!

Eating the ice cream stuck to the lid of the carton

....

I scream, you scream, we all scream for ice cream.

Yes, in terms of **Kitchen Anticipation** not much compares with yanking out a steaming, **freeze-chilled carton** of the cold n' creamy from the back of the freezer. Bowls hit the table, spoons clink on the bench, and the carton starts frosting up as you peel back the lid.

Stare deep into the light pink swirls, **cookie dough chunks**, or vanilla bean dust looking up at you, but just before you plant your spoon deep into the silky smooth layer make sure you scrape off the milky fresh and creamy bit stuck to the bottom of the carton lid.

It's your ice cream appetiser.

AWESOME!

Getting the armrest at the movie theatre

Movie theatres sure are trying.

Let's see, they made the seats taller, screens bigger, **cushions comfier**, and gave cup holders permanent status. They want us to sit back, relax, and enjoy a nice, quiet evening in our perfect seats.

There's just one problem, though: **that armrest**.

Yes, armrests are the only shared space between you and **Hairy-Forearm Frank** on your left or **Pointy-Elbow Elaine** on your right. And you can't share that space, you can't go half-sies, you can't do a time-share. People, there can be no **softly rubbing elbows** with a stranger during the trailers, are we agreed? I don't care how friendly the rubbing is, either. It's just not acceptable.

So we're only left with one option, folks.

That's right: Get there early, **eye your prize**, claim that space, and claim it quick. Plant your **sharp, bony elbows** on both armrests and get ready for the most comfortable movie-watching experience of your life.

AWESOME!

Glass

Grab a handful of sand, heat it up to a few thousand degrees, and suddenly, **presto change-o**, whaddaya got? That's right, friend: a handful of glass and one severely burned paw.

Now, how incredible is the fact that glass is made from sand? I mean, think about it: There aren't many things you **can't see through** that turn into things you **can see through**. It just doesn't happen. Water isn't made from mud, radio waves aren't evaporated rainbows, and Crystal Pepsi isn't just a pot of regular Pepsi stirred really fast.

I mean, can you imagine the first time somebody made glass? For a while there's just an old cauldron hanging over a fire with some sand sizzling in the bottom, and then suddenly it's *clink, clink, clink* and **marbles are** rolling around in there. Now, I wasn't around then, but I imagine whoever was had a great story at the bars for a few weeks.

Glass is so solid, stoic, and sophisticated too—unlike that annoyingly pliable and chemical-leaching heathen, plastic. I mean, apparently the empty plastic cottage cheese container you reheat your leftovers in can fill your meal with a **pile of chemicals** that could mess you up. But that's not so with glass, because glass is a solid fighter and isn't going to cry and fall apart at the sight of a few measly microwaves.

So have you ever looked through a window or watched TV? Do you wear glasses, do you take pictures, do you pour **steaming fluorescent liquids** into beakers in chemistry labs? If so, have you peeked into a telescope or microscope when you were in there? If not, have you ever admired the stained glass inside a church, or enjoyed a cold brew in a beer bottle or some bubbly in a **champagne flute**? Is your house insulated with fiberglass? Do your fish swim in an aquarium? I ask you, friend: Are you sitting under a lightbulb... right... now?

And if so, if any of these things, then I say smile, **flash a thumbs-up**, and give some serious props to glass—that durable, industrious, dishwasher-safe friend who's always there when we need it most.

AWESOME!

When you actually manage to split the group restaurant bill to everyone's satisfaction

....

Gut busting with chicken chow mein and nursing a **fried rice hangover**, your frenzied hour of pillaging steam trays has quickly dissolved into a table full of sticky-smeared plates, bloated bellies, and quiet groaning.

Folks, if you're like me this scene is called **The End of The Buffet**, a dimly lit freeze-frame featuring you and your friends lazily sliding in chairs with slack jaws and heavy eyelids.

And it gets worse too.

The chipper waitress drops off the bill and everybody just eyes each other suspiciously. Who owes who money? Who ordered drinks and who didn't? Is anyone riding a **fat paycheck high** and feeling generous? Since **I am an extremely cheap person**, I generally choose this exact moment to skedaddle to the bathroom in the hope that everyone else will overpay and allow me to just **drop a fiver** on the stack before heading out.

Of course, it never works out that way.

Instead, I return to an untouched bill and generally get pegged as **Math Guy**, also known as **The Job Nobody Wants After Dinner**. See, my friends start chatting about what movie to see and I'm suddenly stuck with my head down, brows furrowed, figuring out tips, collecting cash, and trying to follow the paper trails.

If you're hanging out with me and my friends then Math Guy is a doubly terrible job because **we're always forty bucks short**. People shrug, eye contact is avoided, and there are some phantom wallet reaches, until we figure out that two people didn't add tax and tip and one guy still needs to get cash from the ATM.

Holler if you been there.

Math Guys and Math Girls of the world, we feel each other's pain. It's tough asking people to put more money in and sometimes we just reach into our own wallets to get the job done. Twenties are broken, **coins are counted**, and there is constant checking and rechecking that it all adds up right.

Yes, if you're picking up what I'm putting down, then you know that moment of quiet satisfaction when you finally close that **sticky, sauce-smeared billfold** over a stack of crumpled bills and sliding coins.

Because at that exact moment the shackles of Math Guy are finally busted.

And we're all free.

AWESOME!

A perfect squeegee job at the petrol station

....

Drive that steaming rust bucket up to the pumps and let's get down to business.

Folks, you know it and I know it: Perfect squeegee jobs are hard work. You're a pro wiper if you master these top five tricks:

1. **Lift-ups.** Not everyone has the moxy to wipe under the windscreen wipers, but that's where you'll find dried leaves and lots of highway grime. Don't be afraid to get in there.

2. **Just enough drips.** Okay, if you're pulling the squeegee out of that dirty blue liquid and slapping it on your rear window in one swift move, then you're probably overdripping. There's no need to get your shoes wet, so do like the pros and tap off before you tap on.

3. **Say no to streaks.** Quick wiping is sloppy wiping. Avoid streaks at all costs by using two hands, leaning your head in, and applying just enough even pressure to keep the squeegee running straight. If

you get a streak by accident, it's time to do it again. If you start to compromise, you'll just hate yourself later. Be strong.

4. **Bug off**. Pros don't let smeared bug guts get in their way. No, they'll hammer those out with some furrowed brows and furious back-and-forth swiping. Pay tribute to the ladybug's tiny, beautiful life by disposing of its remains at the station instead of driving them back and forth to work for a few weeks.

5. **Side Mirror Superstar**. Everyone thinks they can do the side mirrors, but the truth is they're nearly impossible. Sure, it's a nice idea at first, but then you realise the squeegee doesn't fit well on there and you'll get inconsistent smudge streaks and a black scribbly cloud above your head. Streak-free side mirrors require years of training. Work your way up to them and expect to make lots of mistakes.

Yes, when you nail the perfect squeegee job you're loving it lots. Mum fills up, dad grabs **beef jerky**, and your kid brother runs for the graffiti-covered bathroom that smells like urinal pucks. But you stumble out that van door, stretch your legs, and just casually eye that squeegee stick.

Then you look at your bug-splattered windscreen, nod a little nod, and smile a little smile.

Because you know what has to be done.

And you know how to do it.

AWESOME!

Fitting every last thing in the dishwasher

··

Wedge those macaroni-and-cheese-covered plates, butter-smeared knives, and sticky glasses in there sideways. Stuff in the **really, really old Tupperware** and double-stacked sandwich containers and then balance a crusty casserole dish on top.

Now, if you think you're done, you're not even close.

No, now it's time for the mad dash around the house grabbing **leftover glasses** from the bathrooms and greasy popcorn bowls from the basement. Then you have to come back and rearrange the clinking, clanging mess like a complex 3D jigsaw puzzle. As you whistle the theme song to Tetris, your brain flashes back to the sixth-grade geometry class that prepared you for this day.

Don't stop until everything's jammed, rammed, and crammed.

And then stuff a few wooden spoons in the sides.

And a couple more forks.

And the can opener.

AWESOME!

When the guy at the deli counter gives you a free taste

Walk into a supermarket and you're surrounded by freshly misted lettuce, **bubbling lobster tanks,** and hot croissants rolling out of the oven. With your pupils dilated and mouth watering, there's nothing finer than rolling your **crookedy-wheel trolley** by the deli counter and making some subtle eye contact with the deli man.

We both know that when you're surrounded by fresh food in all directions you suddenly start jonesing for a fix. So you press your hands on the curved glass and gaze longingly at the giant hunks of **pink and salty** goodness shining at you under the bright lights.

You know what to do: Place your order, **reach your hands out,** and get ready for those thinly shaved slices to touch your tongue and send you on a salty trip far, far away.

Also applies to sample biscuits at the bakery.

AWESOME!

When you went to the gym yesterday

....

Because now you can take a break today.
   AWESOME!

Riding on someone's shoulders when you were a kid

Blast off.

Getting a **six-foot liftoff** when you're two feet tall shoots you straight into the stratosphere. Suddenly you're riding **your own personal human** in a bumpy lounge room safari in the clouds. Your nappy-padded butt bounces safely on sturdy shoulders as you giggle and grab fistfuls of hair and glasses while gazing down at the **tiny toy-covered world** you thought you knew.

Yes, your **baby brain** zooms out and gives a sneak peek of the big world you're about to discover: riding wobbly bikes and skinning your knees at distant playgrounds, cruising around after curfew with fresh driver's licences, and staring out tiny aeroplane windows at distant **crisscrossed patches** of your hometown.

Look back on those blurry shoulder rides in those **jungle backyards** and remember the rushing feeling of going way up, **staring way down**, and opening your eyes . . .

AWESOME!

That clicking sound of winding anything up

....

Mmmm, girl.

You know it and I know it: That **zip-zippery sound** of winding anything up is a slow-building crescendo of anticipation. You crank the plastic walking toy, **spin the garden hose wheel**, or twist the egg timer tightly until everything locks and loads. Don't matter whether you're reeling in a fish, **charging a manual torch**, or preparing a set of chattering teeth to walk across the kitchen table, it all feels great.

It's the sound of important work about to start. **It's the sound of important work about to finish.** It's the sound of progress, movement, and clicky little baby steps toward a bigger goal. Soon the fish jumps out of the water, **the torch lights up the campsite**, or the toy teeters across the cold basement floor.

That wind-up clicking scratches a **tiny little itch** deep in your brain and gives a smirky sense of satisfaction when you've twisted till you can't twist no more.

When you build energy up inside whatever you're winding you sure crank yourself up too.

AWESOME!

Picking up something that turns out to be a lot lighter than you expected

It's the shopping bag of paper towels, **the suitcase of socks**, or the moving box of mittens.

AWESOME!

The last couple of hours before the weekend

....

This is known as **The Funrise**.

Chatty buzz fills office cubicles, laughs echo down high school halls, and the **clock ticks** a little bit faster as we all smile and get ready for a couple of big days of

AWESOME!

Correctly guessing the actor voicing the animated movie character

....

Everybody loves cartoons.

Ain't it fun cuddling under the blanket or plopping down on the plushy seats and getting sucked into tall tales about lost clown fish, tough-talking **sharks**, or toys that come to life?

Now, after the movie starts rolling you quickly fall into the **cartoon fantasy** and there's always that moment where a new character enters the story and starts stealing the scene. And everyone recognises the voice and everyone knows the voice, but without a visual it's tough guessing which big-name star is sweating in the studio holding crumpled sheets of paper and wearing giant **Princess Leia** headphones.

That's why it's great when the electrons suddenly go boom in someone's brain and they jump up and scream out a name. Then everyone smiles and laughs and breathes a big sigh of recognition relaxation. Oh sure, sometimes there's **online fact-checking** or the occasional **wait-till-the-credits confirmation**, but how sweet is it when someone just shouts it out and totally nails it?

Pretty sure we all know the answer to that.

AWESOME!

Dropping a glass and then sticking your foot out so it hits your foot and doesn't break on the ground

Hey, now instead of a **sharp, dangerous mess** on your kitchen tiles, you've got a couple of bruised toes, a complete drink set, and a giant, swelling feeling of
AWESOME!

Running for the bus or train and actually catching it

I'm no runner.

Strap a pair of flashy sneakers on me and **snap on an elastic sweatband** and I generally have no idea what to do next.

But when the bus is coming around the corner or the train is pulling into the station, watch out man, because **I am off**. Yes, no matter what I'm wearing, no matter what I'm doing, no matter who I'm talking to, if I see the faint possibility of catching that bus at the last second, then I'm gunning it.

We all know that **Just missing the bus** is something you'd find over in *The Book of Annoying*, that nonexistent netherlist that also features: Finding out your shirt is inside out partway through the day, When the public bathroom only has one slow lukewarm hand dryer, and When the cashier needs to replace the receipt tape in the middle of your transaction.

But when you run and actually catch it, that's a beautiful moment.

First off, it means you managed to wait the absolute **least amount of time possible.** You didn't check your watch four times and constantly stare up the street for the bus to appear on the horizon. No, you put your head down and bolted and ended up hanging around the curb for 0.0 seconds. Not bad!

Secondly, you score a little **Mini Workout High.** Who cares if your cheeks are glowing, your neck's glistening, and you almost twisted your ankle on the footpath? You don't, because you just got some cardio in. Now you can crumble into your plastic orange seat satisfied your arteries shook off some fat chunks from the plate of danishes you ate earlier.

Lastly, you give everyone else on the train some entertainment through the **Horse Race Bettor** effect. See, everyone else sees you walk onto the platform, bug your eyes out, and bolt into Super Businessman as you start your race. It's an adrenaline rush as they cheer you on. Will Dress and Running Shoes Lady squeeze between the newspaper boxes? Will Stroller Mum get her two-year-old up the escalator past Teenage Mobile-Phone Mob? There is drama, there is tears, and there is cheering.

People, when you frantically wave at the driver from fifty feet away, **leap across the platform**, or jump through those slowly closing doors, you made it. Stare up at your fellow passengers, take in a few deep breaths, and smile big with your sweaty face.

You just won a gold medal in being
AWESOME!

When you drive from a rough road onto a smooth one

....

Cruising onto a fresh black road when you've been scraping on top of a rough one is a mighty fine feeling. When you get off that chopped-up construction meat or swerve out of **Pothole Alley**, your tyres are loving you lots. And it's not just that:

1. **Shhhh.** When you slip onto fresh road the background noise fades away and everyone realises they can chat in a normal voice again. It's a nice, relaxing feeling, and it sort of makes your car feel more expensive, like you tossed down a fistful of bills at the dealership for some primo soundproofing upgrades.

2. **Gimme a break.** When you start cruising smooth it's like driving becomes a lot easier. You're no longer swerving past giant dirtholes on the way out of the cottage or being careful not to slip off the pebbly gravel edge beside the ditch. Thinking of giving both your arms a rest simultaneously? Now's a good time.

3. **Mechanic on duty.** I don't know about you, but sometimes when I'm on a rough stretch of road

and my tyres start to make that rawrrawrrawr sound, I convince myself that something's wrong with my car. I know, I know, I'm a real hypocardriac (*hey-ohhhhhh!*). But seriously, folks, doesn't it feel good when you drive onto a smooth road, perk your ears up, and realise nothing's wrong with your hunk of junk?

Driving from a rough road onto a smooth one is a tiny gift to the road-weary. You don't know when it's coming, you don't know how long it'll last, but for a few fleeting moments you smile and relax in a quiet little meditation on wheels. AWESOME!

Reuniting a sock from the Sock Orphanage Drawer with its freshly washed once-lost brother or sister

....

We don't know where you've been. We don't know how you got home. But come here and give us a hug, old friend.

We thought we lost you.

AWESOME!

When your roommate goes away for the weekend

....

Channel surf in your underwear, crank your embarrassing **dance music**, and let the crumb-covered dishes pile up without guilt. Because when you're splitting the bills, the thermostat, and a few hundred square feet, sometimes you just need some space.

AWESOME!

When your laptop or mobile phone is just about to die but you manage to run and plug it in before it completely shuts off

Warning beeps and **flashing battery icons** try hard to get your attention.

To me they're like **death row prisoners** being escorted down a dim hallway with green ceramic tiles and cinder block walls. They're in baggy orange jumpsuits and shackles, hands behind their back, guards on both sides, just screaming for help before they're strapped to the chair.

"I want to live!!! Stop the insanity!!!"

Your heart aches but sometimes there's nothing you can do. You're in a bus on a long ride home or out at a restaurant for a birthday dinner. You forgot to plug them in before you left, so you stare helplessly as the **juice zaps their veins**, the lightbulb dims, and they go quiet and disappear into blackness. You sigh and toss them in your backpack or just hold their heavy, lifeless body in your hands, say some quiet words, and wipe away tears.

Other times you're the **pricey, hard-nosed attorney**, filing a last-minute appeal and rushing down to prison with court-signed paperwork before someone flips the switch. You run into your apartment and plug it into the wall or borrow a friend's car adapter at the last second. At moments like this, there is a celebration as the charge icon flashes on, flashes strong, and breathes in new life.

AWESOME!

Puppy breath

Their tiny fresh breath has been scientifically designed to melt your heart.

AWESOME!

Carrying all the shopping bags in from the car in one giant trip

It's been a long afternoon.

Making a list, checking it twice, heading to the shops for milk, bread, and rice.

Brother, let's face facts: When you finally wheel onto your slippery leaf-covered driveway with a boot full of wet celery, rolling apples, and melting ice cream, all you wanna do is **finish the job quick.**

It's time to put her in park and start **yanking** bag after bag from the boot and holding them with every possible bag-holding body part you got.

First grab the heavy bags of milk and potatoes with one hand and the **orange juice** and frozen lasagnas with the other. Then pile on the fruits, veggies, yoghurts, and be careful with those eggs, careful with those eggs there. Now, while teetering awkwardly with **eight plastic bags** digging into your forearms, just grit your teeth and grab the final bag of bread and cold cuts with your left pinky while squeezing a giant bulk pack of toilet paper under your right armpit.

Now shut the boot and lock the door using only your elbow, chin, and teeth.

Annnnnnnd . . . you're good!

Oh sure, it's not very majestic, but it'll have to do because **there is no way** you're coming back out here again. No, you did your job and now it's time for your spouse and kids to fill the fridge and pantry—so just run in the door, toss the bags on the floor, and scream, "I'm back from the shops!"

AWESOME!

When you fold a piece of paper so it fits in the envelope perfectly

....

Lick and load, people.

Yeah, yeah, sure, we ain't sending out letters much these days but we both know there's the odd time you're forced to **fold n' crease** a piece of paper and snug it tightly into an envelope for some smooooooooth mailing.

Now, if you don't nail it properly you get a **fat wedge** sticking out the top of the envelope and are left with two horrible choices:

1. **The Creasy Jungle.** This is where you unfold and refold your crinkly masterpiece. It's not ideal because there's no hiding your terrible folding skills and you end up with a messy envelope.

2. **The Fat Flabby Fold-Down.** This one's the postage equivalent of attempting an awkward twelve-point turn when your parallel parking job ends up three feet from the curb. When you're rocking the fat flabby, you're bending that top crease backwards really tightly. This gives you a thick n' chunky wedge that barely squeezes in.

Friend, let's be clear: There are issues.

But that's why it's great when you manage to fold that paper tightly and fold that paper rightly so your letter slip n' slides into the waiting envelope's mouth. When you nail it your eyes twinkle a tiny bit, **your smile curls at the lip**, and your swagger shakes at the hip, baby.

AWESOME!

When you're washing the car and it's hose time

Soapy sponging coats your clunker in a thick sheet of bubbly foam. When your brow is sweating and the sloshy pail is dripping all over the driveway, it's time to grab the hose and rinse the job away.

AWESOME!

When a stranger walks by and offers to take a picture of you and the person you're with

You and your **snugglepuss** are cuddling up together.

Maybe you're taking a romantic stroll in the park, leaning on the railing over a waterfall, or camping out at the airport before your big honeymoon flyaway.

It's times like this when one of you grabs the camera and starts taking pictures. Pout those lips, **tilt that neck**, and get into it. Then grab the camera and take pictures of your loved one too. Big toothy smile, casually distracted straightface, whatever the move you're just **freeze-framing** it forever.

Everything is rolling right along, everything's smooth sailing, until it eventually happens.

You want a couple shot.

Sure, first you try the awkward **cheek-to-cheek pose** that involves squeezing your faces together and holding the camera high in front of you with an outstretched arm. And that's not bad until you realise you're taking four pictures to get one that includes your forehead and there's no hope of getting a full-body shot. Nope, you're not getting a cute couple photo today.

OR ARE YOU?

It's a magical moment when a stranger walks by, notices your awkwardness, and chimes in with a quick "Hey, want me to take a picture of you two?" That's when you smile warmly and say sure, before delicately placing your fragile camera in their hands. The funniest part comes next when you teach them how to use it.

"Press this button."

You know, like every other camera.

But honestly, thanks **Shutter Stranger**. Thanks for stopping for a minute to capture our good side. We may never see you again, we may never pay you back, but we want to give you a big shout-out today for your generous gift of capturing our little moment of

AWESOME!

Vacuuming a dirty carpet and hearing all those tiny rocks go through the hose

Since we're lugging the **heavy vacuum** up from the basement, moving couches around, and getting the whole room smelling like hot dirt, it's mighty nice when those rattling **little pebbles** pipe up and let us know it was *alllllll* worth it.

AWESOME!

Walking or riding your bike faster than cars sitting in traffic

....

Have you ever sat in a taxi in traffic?

Just tell me that's not frustrating. Your heart thump-thumps and your anxiety zooms sky-high while you stare at the **fluorescent red toll** slowly ticking upward. Sure, you know you shouldn't watch it, but you can't stop. You fixate your eyes on the tick-tocking numbers while your taxi slowly inches forward through **tight city streets**, at rush hour, in construction, when it's raining.

There is only one thing that can make this scene more frustrating and that is **watching some dude** walk faster than you on the footpath.

Honestly, look at him, strutting his stuff, moseying down the street at breakneck speed while you pay top dollar for slower service. You may as well roll down the back window and **toss your wallet** in the sewer at this point. Yeah, steam's coming out your ears while your face turns red as a tomato.

But for the faster-walking guy, it's a different story.

He just bops along and watches you sweat.

AWESOME!

The extra time you get when the clocks roll back

....

Bass thumping, **heart pumping**, joint jumping, it's a buzzing Saturday night on the dance floor.

And nothing makes that party stronger or that **conga longer** than knowing **Daylight Savings Time** peels our clocks back an hour tonight and showers us all with some **free weekend**.

Yes, when you know **three in the morning** is going to spin back to two again, it's a Free Pass to go waste a perfect hour with friends. So squeeze in some more video games, order off the menu at Drive-Thru, or dance an extra dance with Grandma at the wedding, because we all know you'll get an extra hour of sleep anyway.

So after you spring forward don't forget to fall right back, y'all. 'Cause there's nothing as nice as living things twice.

AWESOME!

When someone holds your keys and wallet in their handbag

....

Hey, nobody likes walking around with **big bulging pockets**. So today let's give thanks to the **Bag Ladies of the World** for their giant handbags and free storage.

AWESOME!

That feeling in your stomach when you go really high on the swings

....

Because now you're finally tall and can look down at the world below you. Gone are those constant views of ankles, coffee table legs, and your family cat's **hollow, piercing eyes.** Now you're zooming up and over gardens, sandlots, and your **baby brother's distant, fading cries.**

Stomach gushing, adrenaline rushing, it's your first taste of the high life.

AWESOME!

Going through a revolving door without having to push

My friend Matt went on a rant over the weekend.

"Do you realise how dangerous revolving doors are?" he began, with big popping eyes, **concerned eyebrows**, and a thick foamstache on his upper lip from the cappuccino he was sipping. "I mean, I'm surprised they're actually left unguarded in public. Don't you think it's a miracle more limbs aren't lost in those things? Crack, there goes your ankle in the doorjamb. Smack, there goes your face against that unrelenting wall of glass."

He nodded his head in little bobs while staring at the serviette dispenser deep in thought.

"I honestly think I might stop using them altogether... while I still can."

I flashed him a thin, understanding smile while silently worrying he was becoming a bit too paranoid. What's next, I wondered—boycotting shoelaces, **avoiding escalators**, carrying a pocket thermometer to dip into drinks before sipping?

Because let's be honest. Revolving doors are part of life: they came, they're here, they ain't going anywhere, you know? Sure, using them safely is important. But that doesn't mean we can't enjoy them. After all, it's pretty sweet coasting through one of them… especially when you don't have to push:

1. **Catching a draft.** Someone's in front of you so their pushing gets the door moving. Just watch out, though—since they leave the door before you, it'll generally slow down fast before you get out. But be patient and let the door turn slowly, friend. You'll make it.

2. **The Invisible Force.** Here's where nobody's around but the door is spinning like mad. Clearly some beefy strongman just whipped it into a frenzy while rushing to catch the bus or something. This spinning beauty sort of resembles that big wheel on *The Price is Right* whenever a guy from the army sent it flying. Careful getting in and then enjoy the speedy ride.

3. **The Self-Starter.** This one's like The Invisible Force, except the slow speed and deep whirring noise tells you the door's running from a power source. Deeply unsatisfying.

4. **Sharing the pie.** This is Matt's worst nightmare. Here's where you squeeze into the door right behind one of your friends. While they push you try to awkwardly speedwalk so the door doesn't clip your heels.

Going through a revolving door without having the push feels like catching the rhythm of the universe. Entering, exiting, it doesn't matter—nope, you just rode the wave of life without crashing into mess of bloody foreheads and shattered wrists.

AWESOME!

The sound of snow crunching under your boots

Dim streetlights cast **blurry shadows** for your cold walk home.

Snow-packed mitts, floppy wool hat, and a drippy, sniffly nose cover your shuddery frame as you shuffle down **empty side streets** on your way to the cozy warmth of your waiting bed. Everything is an eerily pitch-perfect silence buried under a shadowy sheet of bright white. Pine trees sway softly, **Christmas lights flicker**, and the biting air ice-scrapes your frost-nipped nose.

Somehow the solid crunch of your winter boots against the **packed road snow** fills the night with a relaxing and familiar sound that marks tiny little steps of progress toward cuddling up under warm blankets and falling deep asleep.

Like pushing soft drink lid buttons, cracking frozen puddles, or popping a spoon in a jar of peanut butter, the sound of snow crunching under your **salty winter boots** scratches a primal itch that just feels so satisfying.

So stuff your hands in your pockets, curl your head to your chest, and crunch loud and **crunch proud** deep into the dark winter night.

AWESOME!

Taking a break from shaving

I used to be **The Wolf Man**.

At least, that's what a big guy named Fletch used to call me in year ten homeroom. He said it with a **hearty, bug-eyed giggle** while pinching and tugging the soft patches of thin hair extending from my ears to my collarbones.

Now, I wasn't just born The Wolf Man. No, I had to create the identity by first building up the guts to trim my thin, soft moustache and sideburns for the first time. That first shave was a nerve-wracking ordeal, with a fresh razor, a steamy mirror, too much lather, and **too much blood**.

And I guess being around fifteen years old and new to this whole **slicing-the-hair-off-your-face-with-a-knife** thing, I didn't realise that you were supposed to get the whole **neck area** too. So I didn't get the neck area. I completely missed the neck area. So for a good couple of weeks, I walked around high school with a smooth, freshly shorn face and an **untamed, hairy neck area**.

Ar-ar-aroooooooo!

Once I got the hang of it a little while later there was a brief honeymoon phase where I actually enjoyed shaving. The Wolf Man walked in the bathroom and a few minutes later out popped a fifteen-year-old babyface wearing too much aftershave.

It took maybe six months before I got tired of the whole deal. And ladies, I'm guessing you're feeling the burn too since sliding a razor up and down your legs all the time sounds like even less fun.

Nowadays I'm running late before work wishing all my coworkers went in with three days of cheek fuzz. Other times I'm coming home on a Friday night and realising I need to shave before heading out, so it's back to the bowl for me.

This is why it's great taking breaks from shaving.

Shaving breaks let us temporarily escape our civilised social norms and return to our beautifully hairy roots. Got a scraggly **weird beard** growing on the beach? That means you're officially relaxing. Rocking some hairy legs under the track pants? Just enjoying a cozy weekend in the middle of winter.

Sometimes it's great to get away from it all, stop taking things too seriously, and smile and welcome back your inner Wolf Man.

When you get the chance just relax and enjoy those little moments of being your hairy self.

Ar-ar-aroooooooo!

AWESOME!

Getting the last piece of sleep out of your eye

I'm a mess in the morning.

Drool drips down my cheeks, my mouth **hangs open like a mailbox**, and my eyeballs roll around their sockets in slow motion. Hair scraped sideways, underwear bunched and twisted, I dry-swallow and slowly stumble out of bed while trying to form my first thoughts of the day.

Inside my brain a tiny man is **feverishly working a broom** to sweep away all the dusty shards of dream residue so my conscious self can resume control. When he does, some rusty gears are crunched and I groggily shuffle to the bathroom where my **droopy, mashed-up face** greets me like a monster in the mirror.

It's a hideous sight.

Yes, I immediately notice there was a party in Dreamworld last night and those subconscious animals left my place a real mess. Strange puddles pool on benches, **squeezed-up lemon wedges** fill the sink, and cigarette butts litter the balcony. Folks, I'm junked right out, my lips chapped with the corners cracked, my skin dry and flaking, and my mouth loaded with a big set of furry yellow teeth.

Plus, to top it all off my eyes are **nearly glued shut.**

That's right—goop clogs the corners and fills tear ducts with their sharp n' drippy dregs. And let's be honest here: Those **eye boogies** will catch us if we're not careful, showing up unannounced at job interviews, big meetings, and first dates.

We can't have that.

No, there's only one choice and that's to get digging, people. Cast your finger in the starring role of **shovel, rake, and wheelbarrow** and jam it right in there. Hard bits, sharp bits, gummy little squishy bits, just yank them all, with each tiny crumb giving you **a little pick-me-up** when you lift it up and pull it out.

Now that you can see again it's time to clean up the rest of the joint. Yes, with your eyes back in the game nothing can stop you now. So cue the shave, **cut to the shower scene**, and get ready to enjoy your big, beautiful day.

AWESOME!

Picking things up with your feet

Embrace your inner monkey.

Dirty crumpled socks, **dropped Doritos**, rogue pen caps: We see you there. Yes, we see you right in the crosshairs of our toes and we're about to scoop you up with a good old fashioned foot scrunch.

Bending over is overrated.

Picking things up with your feet is

AWESOME!

Interspecies action-figure wars

When I was a kid and played with **He-Man** guys or Transformers, there was always a time when the scale of whatever war I was waging grew beyond the number of figures I had from that set. This meant that I had to throw in other guys to pad the numbers to make sure everything was just fine.

For example, He-Man would help **The Autobots** when Skeletor was bearing down on them with all his henchmen, some bad GI Joe guys, Randy "Macho Man" Savage, and a lone **Captain Planet** villain from a random aunt two birthdays ago.

This also worked for tournaments, pile-ons, and no-holds-barred street races.

You knew the races were getting out of hand when a big **Tonka dump truck** started playing dirty and dumped a half-dozen **Micro Machines** on the carpet to run the Batmobile off the road.

Sometimes my sister got in on it too.

If the **Decepticons** kidnapped Barbie, then Ken would jump on **My Little Pony** to try and rescue her. And if that didn't work, she'd be forced to wheel out the big guns.

Yes, I'm talking about the **Cabbage Patch Kids**.

Oh sure, they were just stuffed dolls, but they were also four times the size of any of my action figures and had **really heavy faces** that were strong as steel. Basically, the game was over at that point because she'd capture all my men and just toss them in the **Easy-Bake Oven**.

And come on, wasn't there something great about those interspecies action-figure wars? Think back and remember sliding across carpets in your overalls, **making spitty sound effects**, and zooming your head into imagination worlds that were so fun, so real, and so

AWESOME!

When you go out for lunch and come back to a way better parking spot

....

Sometimes there isn't much time for the **Lunchtime Scoot**.

Whether it's during lunch period in senior year, between double shifts at the hospital, or wedged amongst meetings at the office, you've really got to get your move on and **get your groove on** if you're going to fill that belly while the clock's clicking.

And let's be honest, there's a lot of ground to cover. Rounding up the troops, picking a destination, getting to the car and driving somewhere, and then **ordering, eating, and paying for the meal** before scooping up the troops again and zipping back in time. I don't know about you, but in the office where I work some people are pros at pulling off the Lunchtime Scoot and others are in **way over their head**.

Of course, the pros got their reputation by following a few basic rules.

First of all, **they leave early**. "Gotta beat the rush, gotta beat the rush," they'll chant before cramming a carload over to the cafe for 11:35 while the grill is still warming up. But hey, no lines, no traffic, and extra TLC for your **pastrami sandwich**.

Secondly, they're big believers in the **Pee On Your Own Time (POYOT)** Principle. Remember when you were five and your parents made you go to the bathroom before leaving the house? The pros expect you to take care of your bathroom break on your own time, so you don't delay the Lunchtime Scoot in any way. Observe POYOT to score a repeat invite.

Thirdly, watch what you order. If everybody is getting the buffet, don't order a **baked ziti** off the menu that takes forever to arrive. By the time your meal comes, everybody else will be finished, shaking their heads and **tapping their watches**. No bakes!

And finally, the pros generally take command when it's time for the bill. They assume the part of Math Guy without hesitation, and sharply point and issue commands at the end of the meal. "Sandy, you had a drink so thirteen dollars, Raj, you upgraded to **sweet potato fries** so twelve, and everyone else owes ten bucks." And don't even try to go to an ATM or pay with a credit card unless you happen to enjoy receiving **Extreme Stinkeye**.

But the best part about dining with the pros is the classic post-lunch finishing move. Yes, I'm talking about scoring a **much sweeter parking spot** when you get back. While everybody else is still chowing down, you're pulling through that puppy and getting ready to sit pretty all afternoon.

Congratulations on scoring **The 12 O'Clock Upgrade**.

AWESOME!

When the free bread they bring you at the restaurant is warm

....

Hot baked, **warm and steamy**, that basket lands on your table and heats up your whole evening. So sniff it up, crack it open, and enjoy smearing some butter over that warm crunchy-n-chewy deliciousness before the main course arrives.

AWESOME!

Taking off your glasses or contact lenses after a long day

How do you spell relief?

Baby, it's gotta be that deep sensation of finally **relaxing your eyeballs** when you pull your specs off at the end of the day. And whether you're resting your **Coke bottles** on the bedside table or peeling your dry contacts out after a long taxi ride, you gotta love that big moment of freedom fresh air.

When you pull off your lenses you can just blink twice, feel that burn, and give yourself a well-deserved **Pre-Dream eyeball massage**.

Because you're finally free.

Now, if you're blessed with **20/20 vision**, and have no idea what us blind folks are talking about, then let me give you the **Top 5 Sorta-Similar Feelings** from other parts of your life. Here you go, Perfect Eyes:

5. **Unbuttoning the top button of your too-tight dress shirt after a long wedding day.** You trucked around town in a strangling tux and tie with your neck sweating and brown-collaring your shirt through

pictures, speeches, and dancing. When you're finally back in the hotel room, just pop off that button and let it all go.

4. **Flipping your belt buckle open after a big turkey dinner.** You packed your stomach with heaping spoons of mashed potatoes, mountains of stuffing, and a boatful of gravy, so when you crack your belt and let your stomach flop on your lap it's time to droop your eyelids and smile a nice, slow openmouthed smile.

3. **Taking your shoes and socks off after a long day at work.** It's hard to beat the feeling of leg hairs straightening out and blood recirculating past the sock elastic imprints in your calves after peeling off a pair of tight socks after a sweaty day at the office.

2. **Untying your corset in your dim candlelit castle tower.** Such sweet relief from a long day of washing your hair in the courtyard well, attending a stuffy dinner with the King, and sitting through hours of poetry with the troubadours in the town square.

1. **Cracking open your ski boots after a day at the slopes and walking around in sock feet.** All the bumps and blisters on your feet finally relax by the chalet fire after being squeezed together in a ski boot jail all day.

Now, if you're still reading you know all these pleasures make life juicy and delicious. So if you're nodding along and **loving these buzzes** then you deserve big ups for loving all the tiny moments of bliss wedged tightly in the middle of your busy days.

So today we give you a recognition you truly deserve. Congratulations on stopping to smell the AWESOME!

The moment at a concert when the crowd figures out what song they're playing

....

Sweaty crowds in **sticky shirts** scream and scramble for better views between songs. Drums kick boom and guitars get tuned just before the bright lights flip up and **flick on**. Everyone slides forward on the beer-slicked floor and as the first notes kick in we all catch our breath.

AWESOME!

That one car that randomly travels with you on the highway for a really long time

....

Highways can be lonely.

See, we're all strapped in and surrounded by glass and metal, **alone in the zone**, at one with the windscreen as we change lanes and hit the accelerator to keep zooming along, swerving between trucks, speeding past strangers.

But it's this secret street solitude that makes it so sweet when you suddenly notice someone cruising the same streets beside you.

Maybe it's a couple of uni students bumping along on a road trip. **Maybe it's a grizzled trucker in a sweaty singlet.** Maybe it's a minivan with bikes on the back heading to the lake for the weekend.

Basically, it's any car you seem to see over and over again on your trip.

"I swear I saw them before," you might think, peeking in the window to confirm it's the same crew. Tattooed shirtless guy with screaming kid in the black Mustang? It's them! Big-sunglasses girls singing in summer dresses? It's them! Slow-rolling seniors smoking cigarettes with the top down in an old convertible? It's them!

Your heart lifts a bit when you realise you've got company. Suddenly there's a **freeway companion** along for the ride. You get to guess who they are and where they're going and smile every time you notice they're still driving along.

Sometimes you lose them for a while and think they're gone. "We had a good run," you say, before steering into the rest stop for petrol and noticing their car outside the cafe. You smile and shake your head as you pull up beside them.

"I knew they wouldn't leave me."

Sometimes you actually witness the departure at a fork in the road. They head north and you head south, so you say goodbye with **headlight flashes or honks** that say thanks for the trip, thanks for the moment, and thanks for the memories.

AWESOME!

An inbox of personal emails when you wake up in the morning

A fresh batch of personal emails is like a **little basket of gold** to start your day.

Grandkids telling you about kindergarten, blurry photos from last night's party, mum asking what you want for your birthday, and **dirty inside jokes** between your closest friends, all piled on top of each other in your private little den of secret conversations.

You smile softly because a page full of personal emails tells you one thing for sure: **People like talking to you.** So pull up your chair, rub your palms together, and get ready to dive in.

AWESOME!

Passing under a bridge on the highway when it's pouring rain

Your windscreen wipers have no idea what's going on as you enjoy a blissful **two seconds** of silence.

AWESOME!

Finding treasures in your spring jacket pocket

Dig deep, baby.

When the weather warms up and the **snow melts down**, it's time to pull out that thin, dusty jacket from the back of the closet and toss it back on.

Now, just make sure you stuff your hands deep in those pockets and see if you can't score some buried treasure that's been held there safely all winter long:

1. **Your favourite lip balm.** You thought she was lost so you bought some cheap impostors from the chemist to tide you over. But now that greasy beauty's back in business, baby—faded packaging, slippery tube, linty plastic cap and all.

2. **A pack of gum with only one piece left.** The top is probably folded down and creased over that one remaining rock-hard rectangle. You can give it to a friend or enjoy the minty molar-shattering experience yourself.

3. **A Good Times receipt.** This is an old crinkly receipt from a great night a long time ago. Maybe it's a birthday dinner, grad party, or wild girls' night out

on the town. When you stare back at that distant receipt and slowly remember where it's from, you'll eventually end up smiling at the memories. Good times.

4. **That one really good pen.** That smooth-flowing ballpoint never gets lost. No, it just goes on long holidays to your jacket pockets, pencil cases, or board game boxes.

5. **A contact lens still in its packaging.** Say goodbye to your blurry winter.

6. **A shrunken orange.** The bad news is you can no longer eat this orange because it's been sitting in your jacket for months. The good news is you get to smell like citrus for a couple of days.

7. **Travel pack of tissues.** Sometimes if those small packs have been sitting for a while all the lint molecules try to escape from their plastic prison. When you zip open your pocket you catch them coating your liner in the middle of their slow and methodical jailbreak.

8. **Random phone numbers.** Sometimes I pull out a piece of scrap paper and there's just a phone number on it with no name, no context, no nothing. I silently curse my lazy former self and spend a minute debating whether or not I should just dial it up to solve the mystery.

So come on—finding buried treasures deep in those jacket pocket caves is a bit like Christmas in the spring. Yes, you score some tiny little presents from your past as you start a **fresh new season** with big beaming smiles and heartwarming reunions with some dear old friends.

AWESOME!

Pulling a weed and getting all the roots with it

Gardening ain't for sissies.

Nope, if you're getting down with the kneel down you know planting flowers, **growing herbs**, and trimming hedges is tough business, baby. Sun's beating wavy rays, **dirt's clumping in your eyes**, and worms wiggle in all directions as you attempt to plant petunias.

Those weeds are the worst of all.

Sharp stems and jagged leaves spread in all directions and slowly smear across the garden—devouring pristine patches of grass and gobbling up innocent tulips.

That's why it's a great feeling when you pull a weed and get all the roots with it.

First you eye it slowly and grab as close to the base as possible. Next you gently **yank and wiggle** it a little bit to lower its defences and loosen it up. Then it's time for the big moment when you quickly pull it straight up and outta the dirt.

Seeing a long trail of **dirty roots** hanging below that weed you just pulled out of the garden?

Say it with me now.

AWESOME!

Driving over a small hill in your car

Let's hit the suburban roller coaster.

When you're a little kid riding backwards in a wood-paneled wagon, there's few things as fun as hitting a **gut-twisting bump** over a little hill on the highway. Or maybe you're at the back of the school bus, bouncing like jumping beans as you ride the waves, laughing with your snot-nosed pals amongst the slippery nylon seats on your way to the Science Centre. Or maybe you're just cruising down dark roads, **slipping through shortcuts**, and winding off the freeway and rolling over those small hills gives you a small lift on your long drive home . . .

Bumps in the road make life more fun.

AWESOME!

The moment of anticipation before the first kiss

....

Stare into those eyes.

Pupils grow wide and **hearts thump fast** as brains jolt and thoughts roller-coaster around. Conversation jumbles and stumbles before **fading into footnotes** as fingers touch and linger, thoughts twist together, and eye contact drifts and sways before catching and connecting as everything goes quiet . . .

AWESOME!

Staying up past your bedtime when you were a kid

....

Nobody likes bedtimes.

Nope, nothing's worse than lying under the covers in hot flannel PJs with **wide, unblinking eyes** while the late autumn sun slowly droops outside your window. As the sky fades to a **burning orange**, the streetlights flicker on, the moon pops out, and eventually the **thin crack of light** under your door flicks to black.

And then you just lie there, staring at the ceiling, flipping your pillow, tossing and turning, aching and burning.

Nobody likes bedtimes.

Come on, whether it's mum chasing a giggling **nappy-clad junior** around the coffee table or dad forcibly finger-peeling video game remotes out of pre-teen paws, it's all the same when you're a kid.

The fun stops when the head drops.

Yes, bedtime is a **secret, locked roadblock** to a magical mystery tour of late night television, dark CBD scenes, and unknown journeys into all things strange, exotic, and sinful.

But it's that buildup and curiosity that make it great when you finally do break on through to the other side.

Do you remember birthday sleepovers when everybody drank Cokes after 9 p.m. and watched R-rated movies? Did you have faraway **Little League tournaments** where parents cracked beer coolers after the game while kids terrorised the hotel whirlpool and sauna? Did you celebrate New Year's with cousins all dancing to Michael Jackson in the basement as the clock counted down?

Staying up past your bedtime when you're a kid is like getting on a rickety **roller coaster** and riding down a dark tunnel heading somewhere you've never been and were always told not to go. But then you find sugar rushes, skinny-dips, **heart-to-hearts**, and nonstop giggles all waiting for you deep in the blackness, just around the bend.

AWESOME!

Those rare moments when you're the only person on the beach

....

Enjoy the silence.

Maybe you're an early bird who goes jogging on the **cool sand** as the sun rises. Ocean waves quietly lap to shore together with twisted messes of **dark seaweed** and chipped seashells as faint orange sunbeams peek over the horizon . . .

Or maybe you're a **sand stroller** going for a quick walk around the bend as the family takes a **final dip** before heading home. Your feet sink into the hot sand as you find yourself alone with washed-up tree branches, **quiet circling gulls**, and a bright pink sunset lighting up the sky . . .

Or maybe you just discover a quiet patch of **secret sandy paradise** where nobody can find you. It's the hidden beach through the cottage forest, the **rocky island** where you rest your canoe, or the cliffside of a hilly highway where you pull over and hike down to the empty shore . . .

Yes, those rare moments when you're **the only person on the beach** make you feel like you're standing alone in front of the universe. Stare up and let your mind drift into the distant neverending sky, fall deep into the thin horizon, and focus down at the tiny grains of sand **millions of years old** covering your feet . . .

Maybe stegosauruses and **dodo birds** and cavemen and cowboys all stood at this same spot staring out the same way at the same wavy water. And maybe future races will stand **at these same places** and feel the same spine-tingling sense of AWESOME!

When your roommate cleans the place while you're away

My friend Peter has a theory.

We were chatting one day when he mentioned he only does housework when his girlfriend isn't home. I thought it was a bit strange but Peter patiently broke it down for me in three big points:

1. **Hugs and kisses.** When his girlfriend shows up after a long day with her fringe sweat-glued to her forehead, she's not always in a great mood. But when she notices all the rock-hard tomato stains scraped off the stovetop and the telltale blue-tinged hint of fresh toilet bowl, her mood cheers right up and Peter scores some love.

2. **Ditch the guilt.** Then there's the big problem with cleaning up when your roommate, boyfriend, or wife is lying on the couch. While you're straightening magazines and vacuuming in front of them, they feel guilty for chilling out. Forget the hugs— this time you're scoring a big sigh, some lazy stinkeye, and a half-assed helper.

3. **Mr Perfect sightings**. Okay, my place is a mess. Sometimes I fall asleep on dirty clothes, use my dryer as a dresser, and leave macaroni-and-cheese dishes in the sink for days. Peter's not as bad as me, but he's no Mr Perfect either. But see, that's just it—the beauty of his plan is that he gives his girl-friend a chance to dream about her boyfriend clean-ing all day. Sure, the truth is that he was probably stuck in Tube World in Super Mario 3 for most of the afternoon, but those clean benches, spotless mirrors, and fresh vacuum streaks give her hope.

Showing up after a long day to a freshly cleaned place is such a great feeling. Toilet paper has replaced the Kleenex in the bathroom and the **rat-sized dust balls** behind the TV have been whisked away. Now you get to enjoy an evening with someone you love in a sparkly new joint.

So three cheers for organised shoes, **three cheers for empty sinks**, and three cheers for your place looking a lot less dumpy. Yes, if you feel this buzz you're living with someone special. So make sure you give them some hugs and kisses.

Or, if they're out right now, maybe go make the bed.

AWESOME!

That moment in a shower when you decide to make it a really long shower

It's a bad scene.

Alarm bells buzz when the **clock clicks six** and I become a barely blinking lump of groggy stretching noises that sound like Chewbacca after he's been shot by Stormtroopers. Honestly, it's a pathetic scene—me lying there with drool stains on my cheeks, deathbags under my eyes, and bent and jagged bedhead.

Eventually I stumble into the shower and feel my eyes burning and begging to return to the cool and shady **Cave of Closure**. But I soldier on, shower on, soap on, and slowly let that hot steam wake me up.

Sometimes I just can't let go.

No, sometimes I enter a little steam dream in the shower and end up slowing down and thinking to myself: **This is good.**

This is really good.

This should not stop.

Yes, in this magic mist of steamy smiles my brain quickly flips into **Nothing Else Matters Mode**, where all other thoughts just wash away in favour of showering a little longer and living for the day.

Hitting that moment in the shower where you decide to make it a really long shower is a great feeling. As the hot water beats down you get to keep nudging that tap a little bit hotter and a little bit hotter to keep the steam swirling and relax into a soothing personal moment of

AWESOME!

Wearing your boyfriend's jumper

Ripped sleeves, **tattered collars**, and faded prints tossed in crumpled piles on the bedroom floor hold meaningful memories of tender touches. Twisting on the couch for a movie, **stirring over the stove at dinner**, or napping together in the park ... all come together to fan the flames of your heart.

Tossing on your boyfriend's baggy jumper feels like you're giving them a hug.

Close your eyes and smell the love.

AWESOME!

Tips

....

"He ate my tip!"

Tara said that with **eyebrow-crinkling rage** while we were out grabbing drinks on a laid-back patio. She shook her head sternly and surveyed our table of **belchy beer drinkers** for support.

We offered none.

In my defence I had no idea what she was talking about, so I just took a sip of my beer and casually wiped my **foam-stache**. When I glanced back at Tara, I saw she was still steaming about something so I tossed her a thin-lipped nod and a flimsy halfhearted response.

"Your tip, huh. Gee whiz, that is really too bad."

I figured we were done on that random topic but she wasn't stopping. No, she slapped her palms on the sloshy metal table covered in soggy beer coasters and squeezed lemon wedges, leaned her head in real close to mine, and popped her eyes out like a **B-grade horror-movie actress** who'd just been axed in the back.

"You know, the tip of my pumpkin pie. He ate the tip of my pumpkin pie! He knows I love tips. I always talk about tips and he just stole it from me. He ate that **perfect, delicious triangle** at the front of my dessert. I was so mad!"

And then I suddenly got it.

Tips.

"Whoa, whoa, whoa . . . what'd you do?" I asked, suddenly sucked into this escalating tale of sugar robbery.

"Oh, you want to know what I did? I'll tell you what I did. **I ate the tip of every single piece of pie left in the dish.** There were seven left and I just scoffed seven delicious tips!"

Now, this really got my attention. What a **feisty little nibbler**, I thought. Some dude jokingly stabs his fork in her dessert and suddenly lightning bolts flicker in her eyes, her teeth start grinding, and her lips curl into a dark clownish smile.

I kind of liked it.

Frankly, we all did. Yes, we all laughed at Tara's tip-eating rampage that sunny afternoon and realised that, well, come on, **tips are great**. I mean, let's think about it for a second here:

10. **Slice of pizza.** Bubbly cheese, crispy pepperoni corners, and tiny drips of hot orange oil swirl around at the centre of the pie. It's the nucleus of the pizza and the core of all taste. There's no danger of uneven sauce coverage here and the crust is nice and thin. Plus, if you're lucky, you could score a cheese dangle, which involves your pizza tip using the power of the melt to snag excess toppings from a nearby slice. And hey, if your tip is the one

getting robbed of toppings here, no worries. You just scrape up bits of cheese and sausage from the rest of the box and toss it on top. Everybody wins.

9. **The top swirl of a soft-serve cone.** Folks in the business know it's an art creating those delicate curls on the top of cones. It's the baby nibble of the cone and a nice tease for the next few minutes. Most of the way down you're licking and biting your ice cream, so that top swirly tip is a yummy appetiser.

8. **Quiche.** If you're in the game for this one, I'm guessing you love that chunky broccoli, salty ham, fluffy egg, and oily crust combo at the front of your slice. Très yummy, yes pas?

7. **First crispy nacho from the top of the tower.** Full-size triangle chip with crisp corners, bubbly cheese, and little salsa puddles, waiting innocently for you to dive in. This here's the tip of the nachoberg.

6. **Diagonally sliced grilled cheese tips.** This is when you cut your grilled cheese into four triangles instead of two halves in order to increase your tip quotient. Also works for toast. (Note: Although this tip is man-made it still counts under current Tips law.)

5. **First sip from a cold bottle of soft drink or beer.** This is the liquid tip and when the first ice-cold bubbles

touch your lips after a long Friday it's a refreshing bliss.

4. **Margarine tub.** There's something beautiful about stabbing your knife into the belly button of margarine after you open the new container. You got there first and have now officially claimed the tub. Feel free to carve in your initials too.

3. **Watermelon slice tips.** Dig your face in there and eat as loud and slurpy as possible. For bonus points do this on a beach picnic table with piles of laughing kids in front of a slowly setting sun.

2. **A giant slab of cheese sitting on a tray somewhere.** I don't bump into fancy cheese trays very often, but once in a while I'll spot one at a New Year's Eve party and suddenly come face-to-face with that untouched tip of rock-hard cheddar or melty Brie.

1. **Cakes.** We saved the best for last. As those tall, wobbly cheesecake towers arrive at your table or you delicately carve out a thick slab of birthday cake at a party, we both know you're eyeing that delicious triangle right up front. And look at it sugar-shining in the light just waiting for you. It's practically saluting and pledging allegiance to your mouth.

So, people, come on. Let's all hold hands here today and remember the many great tips we've enjoyed over the years.

Smile at all those delicious first bites and first sips that surprised your tongue and teased your taste buds with hints of what's to come.

Love tips, love bites, love tips, love life.

AWESOME!

Driving around with the windows down on late summer nights

....

Kids cruise on wobbly bikes, **toddlers race on tipsy trikes,** and you drift deep into the hot summer night. Swerve and curve on **windy roads** as darkness slowly falls and **stars pop out** to reveal a twinkly twilight glow. As you hit the accelerator and drop your windows, the **warm beating rush of summer air** makes you smile and makes everything else in the world just fade away . . . fade away . . . fade away . . . fade away . . . fade away . . .

AWESOME!

Do Nothing Days

It's like a mirage.

You see that distant **Do Nothing Day** coming up on the horizon of your kitchen calendar. You stare at its **white squarey blankness** beckoning you closer and closer and closer. Time moves forward, days march on, and still nothing gets planned on that beautifully perfect patch of nothingness. No homework, **no dinner dates**, no sports practices, no visiting mates. It's just **you and you** sharing a nice peaceful moment of alone time.

When you're lucky enough to score a Do Nothing Day, do yourself a favour and **do nothing**. Give your brain a break and slip into the easy bliss of lying in crumpled sheets, **taking a long bath**, and ordering out for dinner. Ditch the guilt while you swing in a hammock, cuddle with your cat, or curl up on the couch in front of the TV.

Once in a while it's good to enjoy a completely unproductive daydreamy day with a slow smile and no worries.

You earned it.

AWESOME!

A good turnout on your birthday

....

Everybody gets born.

One day you popped into the world a tiny ball of crying wet nakedness and every year since then we've all stopped to celebrate your big day. Birthdays freeze time as you stare back at last year and get ready to celebrate what's coming around the bend . . .

When you're little . . .

There's a buzz in your bones as your entire class revs up for the Saturday-afternoon screamfest at your place. Flashy invites are handed out, RSVPs are phoned in mum to mum, and loot bags are filled with plastic jewellery as the day approaches.

Soon doorbells bing-bong and your basement becomes a rowdy room of snot-nosed three-footers playing duck-duck-goose, usually with a little girl in baggy thick white stockings and a boy with a huge Pepsi stain on his crotch.

Next it's time to unwrap presents and everyone stares with wide eyes as you shred wrapping paper to unveil a new red truck, some video games, and authentically pooping dolls. Then mum comes around the corner with a glowing neon green cake and everyone screams "Happy Birthday" under paper party hats and dim lights . . .

When you're growing . . .

Online invites fly around to help plan a big night with your friends. Flashy outfits are yanked from the closet, loud music starts banging, and drinks are poured at the bar . . .

Suddenly you're a rock star flashing smiles, kissing cheeks, posing for blurry photos with big toothy grins and icy model stares. Tiaras are placed on your head, shots are stuffed in your hands, and your arse gets slapped by old and new friends as all your circles mix together in a boozy dish . . .

When you're older . . .

Dressed up and surrounded by family you smile and blow out a cake full of candles before staring up at a hall full of everyone you know clapping and singing before your sharply dressed son gives a toast to your life . . .

When you're going . . .

As you stare at the flickering candle in the centre of a small cake, your brain washes past grainy images of six-year-olds at bowling alleys, smashing piñatas in parks, and dancing till the lights come up at the bar. You remember unwrapping a new bike, swapping secrets at sleepovers, and stealing kisses with new flames. You remember breakfasts in bed, your first birthday as a family, and getting socks from the kids every year for a decade . . .

Then you weakly blow out the thin candle before lying back in your flimsy nightgown in the white hospital bed. You stare up at your wife, who has tears in her eyes, and she smiles as you rest one of your fragile hands in hers . . . and the other in your grandson's, who stares up at you with wide eyes and a brand new red truck in his hand.

AWESOME!

The Airport Pickup

It's terrible trying to figure out how to get somewhere in a city you've never been before. Strange bus routes, **new taxi systems**, and mazes of complex maps welcome you to your business trip, weekend getaway, or family holiday.

As you arrive at the busy airport you're confronted by a sea of steaming faces. Baggage pickups are packed, customs desks have lines, and you're scrambling to keep your head together as you get your bearings and worry about making time.

That's why it's beautiful when someone you love picks you up at the airport. Yes, when your teenage grandson, **old uni roommate**, or church choir pal offers to rescue you from the insanity it's a beautiful scene.

When you spot them waiting for you it's time to drop that suitcase, **bug those eyes**, and run with your backpack bouncing on your shoulders into a beautiful airport hug. For just a moment everything fades to a distant background blur as you're picked up by an old friend in a new place . . .

AWESOME!

When your pet notices you're in a bad mood and comes to see you

Everybody hurts, sometimes.

Relationships fritz and fizzle, **bad moods steam and sizzle**, and we all have moments when all we want to do is curl up under a blanket until it all goes away.

In tearstained moments of blackness, **when the weight of the world hangs heavy**, there's nothing as sweet as a furry four-footed friend noticing your mood and coming over for a snuggle.

So let your dog curl into your lap or your cat stare **straight into your eyes**, and sniff back those hot salty tears.

AWESOME!

Appreciating the beauty of all your body's scars and scratches

My friend Joey got his face ripped off last year.

Yeah, while staring at his cheek in the mirror a few months back he noticed a **small rubbery bump** below the surface of his skin. Few months, few phone calls, few appointments later he found himself under the knife in a five-hour surgery getting a **chestnut-sized tumour** slowly untied and airlifted out of a knotty nest of nerves in a high-stakes game of **Operation**.

Thankfully he's okay and he's all better and he's managed to bounce over a pretty bumpy hill in life. We were all pretty nervous but he's come out clean on the other side.

Plus, now he's got a **crazy scar** from his ear down to his neck to show for it.

And sure, over the years the stitches will drop out, hair might grow over, and the lines on his face could slowly fade away. But he's really got a reminder **every day** of how lucky he is to be alive. He added some dents and scratches to his life story.

And unless you're a **baby-powder-smelling** ball of smooth skin and giggles, I'm betting your flesh and bones is covered with some gashes, scratches, scabs, and stains too.

Maybe it's that fleshy scar on your hand from the year eight fistfight. You were on the bus back from shop class throwing **pockets of sawdust** around when tempers flared and a couple of headlocks later you tripped and hit the ground.

Maybe it's the ghost of that **Giant Zit of '97** on your forehead. Did you squeeze it too hard before prom and end up with a bad cover-up job? If so, maybe you can still find your old friend in that photo album, wedged tightly between updos, **wrist corsages**, and freshly pressed tuxes.

Maybe it's a **blurry tattoo** you got with distant friends you don't speak to anymore. You were young, you were graduating, you wanted a memento of getting through a tough year together. And you got it.

It's the zippery line up your groin from the hernia, the tingly bump in your collarbone from the monkey bars, or the big birthmark on your back you've hidden under bathing suits for years.

But whatever yours are, **wherever yours are**, and however you got them, one thing's for sure: Your bumps and scratches are part of your life and part of your story. They're part of your lows . . . and part of your glories. They're memories of **bad decisions** and reminders of good ones. And they all come together in a nicely wrapped package that we like to call . . . you.

See, we're all a bit bent, we're all a bit busted, we're all a bit broken, we're all a bit rusted. Underneath all the crinkly jeans and wrinkly shirts are beautifully personal collections of hairy legs, **zippery scars**, and spotty skin.

So take a second to stop today and love all your scabs and patches. Just kiss those moles and **rub those bumps** and smile at all your scratches.

AWESOME!

Getting to the light at the end of the tunnel

My world was spinning in 2008.

After finishing school in Boston and going on a cross-country road trip with my friends Chris and Ty, I moved to a dusty suburb to live with my brand new wife in my brand new life. Yes, we got married young, **we got married quick**, and after living on opposite sides of the border we were finally moving in to **get busy living**.

So I slapped on a crisp, fresh shirt and started a new **office job** while trying to settle into a brand new town where I didn't know anyone. My high school and uni friends had long **scattered like marbles** so I was looking for a new place in a new world.

Now, my wife had been teaching for years so she had a bit more going on. She'd coach **baseball tournaments** and I'd stroll around waving at old folks on their porches. She'd play volleyball and I'd eat biscuits and flip past re-runs. She'd watch *Grey's Anatomy* with friends and I'd practise the fine art of taking long naps and playing video games.

I was feeling pretty lonely and whenever I flipped open a paper the news didn't exactly cheer me up either. Polar ice caps were melting, hurricanes were swirling in the seas, **wars**

were raging around the world, and the job market was in a deep freeze.

It seemed like everything outside my window was just bad and everything inside my window was just . . . sad. Yes, although my wife and I had respect, trust, and admiration for each other, it was becoming clear after a few months that . . . something was missing.

So one chilly spring night in 2008, alone in our dark house, feeling cut off from the buzzing world of bright lights outside, I went online and on a whim started up a tiny website called **1000 Awesome Things.** I wanted to try to focus on the positive by writing about one awesome thing every night after I came home from work.

I think I needed to remind myself there were bright spots in the darkness. I think I needed a cold breath away from the **hot swirling clouds** around me. I think I needed a place where I could smile at the little things we all smile silently at throughout our days.

Over time our nights at home grew a bit quieter, **our dinners a bit shorter,** and our laughs faded into polite smiles. While the year rolled on, we kept living together but were growing further apart. She'd coach badminton and play on her volleyball team and I'd stay home writing for hours about **picking perfect nachos** and the smell of gasoline.

We kept trucking, kept slugging, kept soldiering on, until the rubber finally hit the road **one quiet night** while we were sitting on the couch. She looked me straight in the eyes and through painful tears summoned the courage to tell me she didn't love me anymore.

It was heartbreaking.

Tears spilled all weekend and wet pillows, **sweaty blankets**, and head spins came in waves. By Sunday night I blinked **bleary-red eyes** and suddenly realised I didn't have anything to write about except crying. So that's what I did and that's why that Monday-morning entry is in *The Book of Awesome*.

When I think back to that time I'm reminded of heavy moments at the bottom of a dark well staring way, way up at the **tiny pinprick of light at the top**. But I'm also reminded of the joy and relief of letting awesome things cheer me up while I struggled to keep moving.

I guess I'm addicted to letting thoughts of crunchy leaves, **shopping trolley rides**, and pizza slice tips swirl in my head and lift my brain sky-high. I love talking with all of you and reminding ourselves of the many awesome things we all have to share.

For us, we just happened to be **two different people** walking two different paths. Sure, it was painful as painful can be, **but we need to grieve**, we need to let emotions overcome us, and we need to choose to walk toward those bright lights in the distance. Even if those lights seem pretty far away.

So, come on: When bad news squeezes your lungs and the weight of the world **pushes you under**, let's always try to catch our breath by focusing on the best things in life. Yes, let's focus on the sound of steaks hitting a hot grill, **taking the**

price tag off in one quick move, and good turnouts on your birthday. Let's focus on beautiful pick-me-ups like getting the airport pickup, laughing with friends till you cry, or holding the keys to your first apartment. Let's focus on all the magic moments, eye-twinkling memories, and small special touches that make every day so sweet and make every day worth living.

Yes, life's too short to swim in the deep forever, so **when it hurts** remember to focus on the end of that tunnel and let those lights guide you forward and forward and forward and forward and forward and forward and forward.

AWESOME!

ACKNOWLEDGMENTS

And away we go!

To **oxygen**, thanks for being breathable. To **trees**, thanks for making oxygen. To **Earth**, thanks for making trees. To **the universe**, thanks for making Earth. To **The Big Bang**, thanks for making the universe. I love you, The Big Bang.

To **Sam Javanrouh**, thank you for taking such stunningly beautiful photos for this book. For those as addicted to Sam's photos as I am, check out his site at www.dailydoseofimagery.com.

To **Frank Warren of PostSecret**, thanks for your guidance, support, and friendship. And thanks for being you. You're the only you I've got.

To the one and only **Chad Upton**, this book wouldn't have happened without you. Almost nothing in the world is as rock solid as your endless friendship and I can't thank you enough for the support, ideas, and strength.

To the **'92/93 World Series champion Toronto Blue Jays**, thanks for showing a little kid with thick glasses, wide eyes, and a messy haircut that dreams really can come true.

To **Shiv**, **Dawn**, **Julie**, **Nick**, and **Rita**, thanks for dim nights, late nights, and lots of brainstorming.

To **dark chocolate, Granny Smith apples**, and **guacamole**, thank you for being tasty and delicious. Same goes for you, **poutine**. I admit I dream about your gooey cheese curds, dark steamy gravy, and hot, slippery fries a little too much.

To the **readers of 1000 Awesome Things,** thank you for your passion and soul. Special shout-outs to **Laura Johnson, Bekah Martin, Jennifer Durley**, and **Fred Thate** for their bear-sized hearts and neverending love.

To **Agostino** and **Natalie Mazzarelli**, thank you for having beautiful babies which are fun to finally get the perfect picture of.

To **sentences ending in of**, I think you get a bad rap. Frankly, you do a fine job, if you ask me. Nope, nothing wrong with a good sentence ending in of.

To **Kevin Groh**, your creative ideas have helped spread awesome everywhere. This is your fault. Remember that.

To **Mike Jones**, you've been inspiring me since Dog Guy. There's so much of you in this book. Never change.

To **Erik Lundgren**, thank you for your bright lightbulb ideas.

To **Heather Reisman, Joel Silver**, and the gang at **Indigo**, thank you sincerely for your endless support and always believing in awesome. It's been an absolute pleasure getting to know you all.

To **John Montagu, Earl of Sandwich**, thank you for inventing the sandwich.

To **David Lavin**, **Charles Yao**, and the folks at The Lavin Agency speaking bureau, thank you for sending me to meet awesome believers everywhere.

To **Collin and Abigail**, thank you for the "1000 Awesome Things" song. And to **Mr David Thompson** (Monsieur Cabinet), thank you for the pretty pictures.

To **Matthew, Liz, Kate, Lydia, Amanda, Sharon**, and everyone at **AEB/Putnam**, thank you for your faith and support. It's been an absolute pleasure working with you all. High fives to **Ivan Held, Scott Loomer**, and the one-and-only **Beth Lockley** for their spirit, flair, and energy.

To my editor, **Amy Einhorn**, you're my favouritest favouritest. Your passion has guided this from the beginning and I'm forever grateful. And to **Halli Melnitsky**, you are kind, passionate, and strong. Keep pushing.

To **Erin Malone**, I can't thank you enough for your guidance, support, and putting-up-with-me-ness. You've changed my life and I'm forever grateful.

To **Gale Blank**, **Jim Thompson**, and **Duncan Mac Naughton**, thank you for your optimism and encouragement.

To **Gary Johnston**, thank you for listening.

To *Willy Wonka and the Chocolate Factory*, thanks for being my favourite movie when I was growing up. Don't worry, *Pee-wee's Big Adventure*, I love you too.

To **anyone who's ever given an inspiring commencement speech**, man, I love those. Thanks so much.

To **Dave Cheesewright**, yõu're the ultimate inspiration.

To **Vanessa Crandall**, thanks for making my english gooder. I wish you where around to proofread my Acknowledgments.

To **computers**, thanks for letting us all talk to each other. Please don't take over the Earth.

To **Chris Kim**, you've taught me that some friendships keep growing when they're gone. Your strength fires me up daily. I miss you and love you.

To **luck**, thank you so much. I was lucky to be born healthy in a great country, have parents who loved me, teachers who cared about me, and friends who supported me. If you're reading this, maybe you're lucky too. Maybe we're lucky together.

To **Leslie Richardson**, thank you more than you can know.

To **mom, dad, Nina, and Dee**, you gave me everything I've got and this is very much for you.

Finally, thank you to **you**. Thank you for reading this sentence. And this one. And this one. And thank you for the great chat about awesome things. I had so much fun and look forward to our next one. Now, let's go play outside. The sun is shining, the grass is twinkling, and there's still a couple hours before sunset . . .

ABOUT THE AUTHOR

Neil Pasricha gets stuck in traffic jams, eats entire tubs of ice cream in one sitting, and has terrible posture. He's just a regular guy who loves sneaking candy into movies, stomping crunchy leaves on sidewalks, and watching milk go into coffee.

My Awesome Things

_____

_____

_____

_____

_____

_____

_____

_____

_____

_____

_____

AWESOME!

WHAT'S YOUR AWESOME THING?

Let's keep the awesome going! If you'd like your awesome thing to be considered for use on www.1000awe somethings.com, just write up something less than five hundred words and send it over. We'll pick some favourites and mail those selected a basket of awesome goodies for your troubles. Go to the website to see how to submit. Thanks for reading, thanks for sending your thoughts, and thanks for being

AWESOME!